MAINE HIKES
Off the Beaten Path

35 TRAILS WAITING TO BE DISCOVERED

Aislinn Sarnacki

Down East Books

Camden, Maine

Dedicated to Derek and Oreo, the best hiking buddies a girl could ask for

Down East Books

Published by Down East Books
An imprint of The Rowman & Littlefield Publishing Group, Inc.
4501 Forbes Blvd., Suite 200
Lanham, MD 20706
www.rowman.com

Distributed by NATIONAL BOOK NETWORK

Copyright © 2018 by Aislinn Sarnacki

Maps: © 2018 The Rowman & Littlefield Publishing Group, Inc.

All photos by Aislinn Sarnacki

British Library Cataloguing in Publication Information available

Library of Congress Cataloging-in-Publication Data available

ISBN 978-1-60893-598-7 (paperback)
ISBN 978-1-60893-599-4 (e-book)

∞™ The paper used in this publication meets the minimum requirements of American National Standard for Information Sciences—Permanence of Paper for Printed Library Materials, ANSI/NISO Z39.48-1992.

Printed in the United States of America

The author and Rowman & Littlefield assume no liability for accidents happening to, or injuries sustained by, readers who engage in the activities described in this book.

Contents

Introduction

Sitting in the back of the pickup truck, I held my backpack tight to my chest, nervous about the long and strenuous trek ahead. I was 16 years old and I was joining family and friends to climb Katahdin, Maine's tallest mountain. Topping off at 5,267 feet above sea level—that's nearly a mile high—Katahdin is considered one of the most challenging hikes in the state, if not *the* most challenging. The average round-trip time for the hike is 10 hours, and the total elevation gain is around 4,000 feet. And it was my first major hike.

The truck bed vibrated and jumped under my running sneakers as we navigated down the gravel park road toward Roaring Brook Campground. Trees crowded in on both sides—green walls of a forest so dense, I felt as if I were in the jungle, in another world entirely. I gripped the edge of the truck bed and stared ahead, glad for the trees, grateful that they blocked out that monster of a mountain. I'd seen it the day before, its long jagged ridge lording over the park, and I couldn't imagine climbing to its peak. It seemed impossible.

Though inexperienced in hiking at the time, it was my good fortune to be hiking with family and friends who had hiked Katahdin many times before. That day, their encouragement and guidance helped me have a successful hike to the summit at Baxter Peak and back down to the group campground at the base of the mountain. That night, I slept soundly, and the next morning, I ached all over.

A few weeks after the hike, the toenails on my two big toes blackened and fell off—the result of wearing running shoes and not clipping my toenails short before the hike. And while I did return to Baxter the following summer to hike with my family, I was far from hooked on the activity. I considered it to be something I did one or two times a year, and I only knew about the state's most famous mountains—namely Katahdin and Cadillac.

It wasn't until I was in college that I considered what hiking could do for me personally. I was working at a local outfitter at the time, and I think that may have planted a seed. I was constantly helping customers select hiking boots and water filters, camp stoves and backpacks. And when things got slow at the store, I read the hiking guides for sale on the bookshelf.

Then I started to go through a tough time. I got sick. It's a long story, one I hope to share sometime through writing, but for the purpose of this introduction, I'll simply say that I struggled and was diagnosed with clinical depression and anorexia nervosa. With a great network of support from family and friends, I fought back and regained my health, and connecting with the outdoors played a huge role in my recovery. While I attended counseling, took medication, and worked toward creating healthier habits, I also started hiking on a regular basis, often alone. I started with small hills, and as I gained back my strength, I tackled more difficult trails. For me, hiking went from being a once- or twice-a-year thing to an activity that greatly contributed to my overall well-being.

Wanting to share the experience with others, I wrote an undergraduate thesis for the University of Maine Honors College about hiking and the positive ways the activity can affect a person's physical, mental, and emotional health. I then graduated from the University of Maine with a bachelor's degree in journalism and went on to work for the *Bangor Daily News*, now known as the BDN.

I started as an intern on the copy desk—editing stories, writing headlines, and organizing pages. But I wanted to write, so when a full-time writing position opened up, I applied and got the job. My "beat," or assigned topic, was arts and culture, though I'd often write for the Outdoors section on the side. That evolved over the years to me writing almost exclusively about the outdoors, and more specifically stories about wildlife, conservation, and outdoor recreation.

In 2011 my editors asked me to start one of the first BDN blogs, on which I'd post a series of weekly videos and columns. A bit overwhelmed, I searched for a topic, something I knew that I could write about, photograph, and film every week. I chose something I was passionate about. I chose hiking.

Over the next six years, I visited and reported on nearly 300 trails throughout the state of Maine. To BDN readers, I became "that hiker girl," and through the many pathways of the Internet, I connected with hundreds of fellow hikers and nature lovers from Maine and beyond.

In the fall of 2017, my editors at the newspaper decided that they needed me to focus on different types of outdoor content, to expand my horizons and reach new readers. My first reaction was something like, "But I'm not done yet. I haven't hiked all the trails in Maine." But that's just silly. I'll likely never hike all the public hiking trails that exist in this giant state. Or maybe I will, but it'll take a lifetime. And just when I think I've covered them all, a land trust will conserve another chunk of land and construct a beautiful new trail for everyone to enjoy.

I also realized that I didn't need to stop hiking just because my employer required new content from me. Hiking is what most people do in their free time, after all. So I would keep hiking, keep exploring new trails, and keep recording them because— let's be honest—I just can't stop. I enjoy making videos, taking photos, and writing about my adventures. So I'd do that, too, on my own time.

People often ask me how I find so many different trails to explore, and the answer isn't simple. There isn't one resource for learning about all the trails in Maine. Instead, I gather my information from many guidebooks, websites, brochures, and mobile apps. Over the years, I've discovered new resources, which very often include tips from my readers, and with them new trails—or at least new to me.

The main reason trail information is scattered in Maine and elsewhere is because so many different types of landowners build trails and open them up to the public. When I first started my column, I visited a lot of state parks because they're so easy to find, online and on the road. I also did a lot of hiking in Maine's famous Acadia

National Park, and that led me to look for more federally conserved land and trails through the US Fish and Wildlife Service.

It wasn't long before I discovered Maine's many land trusts, small organizations that conserve properties all over the state. With the help of hundreds of volunteers, these land trusts build some amazing trails, and they're usually free for the public to access. I also learned that most of these land trusts can be searched online through the Maine Land Trust Network.

In addition to surfing various land trust websites, I often check out trails built and maintained by the Maine Audubon, the Nature Conservancy, the New England Wildflower Society, the Maine Appalachian Trail Club, Maine Huts & Trails, the Appalachian Mountain Club, the Forest Society of Maine, and many other organizations.

Then there's Baxter State Park, the place where I was introduced to hiking. Even after six years of exploring those trails, I still have many I've yet to hike in this amazing park. It's the perfect example of how many hiking trails are in Maine, right under our noses. In Baxter, most visitors are focused on one mountain—Katahdin. But did you know that the park is home to more than 40 other peaks as well as trails to ponds, lakes, and other interesting destinations?

Gifted to the state of Maine by Percival P. Baxter, governor of Maine from 1921 to 1924, Baxter State Park consists of more than 200,000 acres of some of the state's most mountainous terrain. "The park will bring health and recreation to those who journey there," Baxter stated in 1921 while proposing the park to the Maine Sportsmen's Fish and Game Association.

When it comes to me, I know Baxter was right. To date I've hiked Katahdin more than a dozen times on various trails. I've also hiked some of the park's other mountains, including the Owl, OJI, the Brothers, Mount Coe, Doubletop, North Traveler, South Turner, and some less-traveled ones such as Sentinel and Trout Brook, both of which I've included in this guide.

In Baxter I've pitched a tent, cooked over a fire, played cornhole, and bathed in ice-cold mountain streams. I've found "health and recreation" and a whole lot more. I hope this book helps you do the same, in Baxter and many other outdoor destinations throughout Maine, and introduces you to a few trails and outdoor organizations that you didn't know about before, inspiring you to get out there, off the beaten path.

Leave No Trace: The Wonder behind the Words

On the longest day of the year, summer solstice, I stood on the banks of Abol Pond and took a deep breath. The breeze off the water drove away the mosquitoes. Orange and pink bled across the sky as the sun sank behind the mountains of Baxter State Park. As I watched a dragonfly light from one grass blade to the next, I wondered about the importance of all the things I'd learned that day. Would the lessons change the way I acted? Would I ever share the knowledge with others?

I would stay in the park that night, my bed a thin pad and sleeping bag, tucked in a small tent. The next day, I'd further my education in Leave No Trace outdoor ethics. All of us—five students and two instructors—would work together to become better stewards of the wilderness we love so much.

"Leave No Trace." You've seen the phrase at trailheads and park ranger stations; in outdoor newsletters, pamphlets, and maps; on bumper stickers and Nalgene bottles. It is the most widely accepted outdoor ethics program used on public lands. But what does it really mean?

When I was invited to participate in a two-day Leave No Trace trainer course in Baxter State Park a few years ago, I decided it was a good time to find out.

Prior to the course, I received a packet for trainees and learned more about the Leave No Trace Center for Outdoor Ethics, a nonprofit organization with alliances to the National Park Service, US Forest Service, Bureau of Land Management, and US Fish and Wildlife Service. The course would focus on the seven Leave No Trace principles:

- Plan ahead and prepare.
- Travel and camp on durable surfaces.
- Dispose of waste properly.
- Leave what you find.
- Minimize campfire impacts.
- Respect wildlife.
- Be considerate of other visitors.

I practiced the first principle by packing everything they suggested on their course equipment list, including a cookstove, headlamp, compass, whistle, sleeping bag, and bug repellent—plus a few extras items: a book for bedtime, beef jerky, and a camera.

After a video, lecture, and lunch at the Baxter State Park administrative offices in Millinocket, we headed into the park to set up camp at Abol Narrows Campground, where we erected our small tents in the campground's lean-tos to minimize our impact on the ground. That evening, we sautéed green peppers, eggplant, and onions over a tiny gas cookstove. On another stove, we boiled water for rice and beans. On a picnic table, the rest of the crew cubed cheese, sliced tomatoes, and gutted avocados.

Exercising Leave No Trace practices, we draped a tarp over the picnic table for easier cleanup, and we washed our dishes 200 feet—about 70 steps—from our tents to prevent nuisance animals from swarming our sleeping area that night.

About 60,000 people visit Baxter State Park each year, a number that is only increasing. And as more people visit parks, land trusts, and wildlife refuges, their impact has a cumulative effect on the wildlife of those areas. That's why knowing and teaching Leave No Trace principles is more important today than ever.

That first day of training, we learned about the principles and why they're in place, but the second day was different—it was spent putting those outdoor ethics into action. Through discussions and skits, our small group learned that it's one thing to know the seven principles and another to make decisions based upon them. That second day, we talked about how we feel about the wilderness, because in the end, while outdoor ethics are built from experiences and education, it's your personal beliefs, your convictions, and your inclinations that put those ethics into action in the solitude of the wilderness, in the company of white pines and mossy boulders. It comes down to how you feel—how your actions in the privacy of a quiet forest rest upon your conscience.

Those seven principles are just words without ethical thinking to put them into action; and ethical thinking is largely based in emotion, in conscience, the eerie feeling you get when you know something is simply wrong.

To best explain, I'll go back to Abol Pond on the summer solstice, and I'll bring you with me.

Your feet sink into a springy bed of pine needles as a warm breeze ruffles the water. A loon calls in the distance. Dragonflies zip over lily pads, and the setting sun paints the sky such marvelous colors that you could never accurately describe them in words. The wonder of the moment is overwhelming.

Now imagine the initials *AJ* carved into a white pine to your right, a cigarette snubbed out by the trunk. Picture a soda bottle floating in the shallows, bumping up against the bank. Noisy campers drown out the call of the loon. And ask yourself if any of that bothers you.

If it does, you get it. Leave No Trace.

Staying Safe while Hiking

I was in college when I started to really get into hiking, and more specifically, solo hiking. And ever since, my family has expressed their worry about my personal safety while I'm out tromping about in the wilderness. "What if you get lost?" they ask me. "What if you run into a dangerous person on the trail? Or encounter a bear? Or break a leg?"

Their concerns are valid. Hiking, like any activity, involves risks. But when people drill me about the potential dangers of the sport, here's what I say: For me, the benefits of hiking far outweigh the risks or dangers associated with the activity. Compared to a lot of other activities—such as driving a vehicle—hiking is safer. And most importantly, I do what I can to minimize the risks associated with hiking.

Over the years, as I've spent more time on Maine trails, I've learned different ways to minimize risks. For the most part, I learn through direct experiences, which often involves making mistakes. But sometimes, I'm lucky enough to learn a thing or two from more experienced outdoors people. So before you hit the trails described in this book—many of which are fairly remote and challenging—here are a few ways I've learned to hike more safely.

Plan and Prepare

I'm the type of person who enjoys spontaneity, but when it comes to going on an outdoor adventure, I find that a little preparation ahead of time can make a significant difference in how much I actually enjoy the outing.

A part of planning and preparing is packing the right gear and wearing the appropriate clothing. For a day hike (a hike that doesn't require any camping because it can be completed in one day) a good rule of thumb is to pack enough in your backpack to spend a night in the woods. It sounds like overkill, I know, but I didn't say a "comfortable night"—just enough to survive and keep your wits about you. The reason for this is, if some misfortune befalls you—perhaps you sprain an ankle or become lost—people probably won't notice you're missing until late in the day, after you are due to return. At that point rescue teams will mobilize, and it may take them some time to find you. You'll likely spend the night in the woods, and if you have the right gear, it's not that big of a deal.

One thing I like to carry with me is an emergency blanket, a heat-trapping tarp that folds into a tiny square but can really help you stay warm if you're stuck in one spot overnight. Essential items in my backpack include a small first-aid kit, a headlamp with extra batteries, a fire starter, a compass and map, a multitool, and plenty of food and water. Other items I often take along are a GPS device, a charged cell phone (though don't count on reception in the Maine woods), emergency water purification tablets, electrolyte powder, Benadryl in case of an allergic reaction, a whistle, insect repellent (especially during June and July), extra layers of clothing, sunscreen, and biodegradable toilet paper.

Share Your Plans

Once you've made a plan, it's extremely important you share that plan with one or more people (preferably responsible people). Give them detailed information about where you're going and when you expect to return. In fact, write it down for them (or text it to them), just in case it slips their mind. That way, if you don't return, they'll know where to start looking. In Maine, it's the state game wardens who lead searches for missing people on the water and in the woods. If it comes to that, you're in good hands.

Dress Smart

When it comes to dressing for a hike or any aerobic activity, try your best to avoid cotton, which absorbs your sweat and dries slowly. Wet clothing can be extremely dangerous when you're out in the wilderness, especially if you're hiking a mountain, where the temperature usually drops as you gain elevation. In addition, atop a mountain, you are usually exposed to wind, which can make a huge difference in your body temperature.

Hypothermia—the condition of having an abnormally low body temperature—is one of the top dangers of hiking in Maine. As someone who hikes year-round, I'm especially cognizant of that danger when I'm planning winter hikes, but it's not just a winter issue. A Baxter State Park ranger once told me that people have become hypothermic in the middle of the summer while hiking in the park.

So if you can't wear cotton, what can you wear? Synthetic materials such as polyester, nylon, and rayon are all good choices. If you check the tags of outdoor clothing, you'll see that these materials are often blended with cotton. That's OK. Just look for a blend in which the synthetic materials are at a higher percentage than the cotton. Another good material for hiking is wool, and for people with sensitive skin like me, specifically soft merino wool. These materials will help you stay dry and comfortable while you hike, no matter what time of year.

Also, dress in layers. That way, if you get hot and start to sweat, you can remove a layer of clothing. For example, in the winter I typically wear merino wool long underwear (top and bottom), a fleece jacket, snow pants, a windproof coat, wool socks, mittens (preferred over gloves), and a hat. If I start to get hot, I take off my hat, then my coat, then my mittens, then my fleece. And if I start to feel cold, I put those layers back on.

You can also bring extra clothing with you in your backpack. This is most useful when you get to the top of a mountain and your shirt is soaked through with sweat. If you have a dry shirt in your backpack, you can change and be that much more comfortable on the way down the mountain. Also, when hiking a large mountain, I always bring a rain jacket, which also acts as a windbreaker. You might be surprised how much colder it is atop a mountain than it is at the trailhead. Extra wool socks can also come in handy.

Spoil Your Feet

In addition to wearing good wool socks, it's important you take the time to select the right footwear. Having comfortable, quality boots can significantly minimize your risk of getting injured in the woods, especially in Maine where the terrain is naturally rocky, frequently wet, and covered with exposed tree roots. In other words, in this state, there's a lot to trip and slip on.

I used to work at a local outfitter, and my favorite merchandise to sell was hiking boots and running sneakers. I loved helping customers find the right footwear, and the first thing I'd ask them was: "What are you going to be doing in these shoes?"

Different footwear is created for different activities. For hiking, I usually prefer to wear hiking boots, and I'm not being sarcastic. I've seen plenty of people hiking in sneakers, tennis shoes, and even sandals. I've seen people hiking rocky mountain trails barefoot, in fact. But when it comes to my feet and my ankles, I know that I am much less likely to fall down if I wear high-topped hiking boots with sturdy soles. I also look for boots with good traction and what's known as a "true heel": the heel of the boot forming a 90-degree angle that can catch tree roots and rocks if you slip forward on the trail. I also opt for waterproof boots, usually with GORE-TEX lining, because Maine is such a wet state. And I take into consideration the weight of the boot. If two types of boots seem to be similarly comfortable and supportive, it makes sense to choose the boots that weigh less. There's no point carrying more weight than you have to on the trail.

I could go on and on about hiking boots, but my main message here is to take your time selecting your outdoor footwear, whether it's hiking boots or water shoes or trail running sneakers. Everyone has their own preferences, and everyone's feet are different. Some footwear brands are better for narrow feet, while others are great for wide feet. Some people hike better in boots with flexible soles, while other hikers are more comfortable in stiff-soled boots. Listen to your feet, consider your activity preferences, and go with what feels right. And if you're going to splurge on any piece of your hiking gear, make it your footwear.

Study the Trail

Now that you're packed and dressed, it's time to find the best trail map possible for your adventure. Some trail maps are available online through trail maintainer websites, while others are only available in certain print resources such as brochures or guidebooks. However you get ahold of a map, make sure you carry it with you on the hike. You won't be sorry. I refer to my trail maps several times throughout my hike to pinpoint where I am on a trail and make decisions. If you don't know how to read a map, it may be handy to take a class or an online tutorial. It's not that difficult, and it can actually be a lot of fun, not to mention empowering.

With a map, it'd be wise to know your way around a compass. From plenty of experiences, I've learned that a GPS device tends to fail a lot more often than a simple compass. After all, batteries drain and freeze. Maybe it's a bit old-school of me, but I find that the simpler the tool, the less likely it will break.

Know Your Body

Once you've planned and prepared for your hike, you should feel confident on the trail. But don't get too carried away. A great way to stay safe in the woods is by taking the time to learn your physical and mental limits. For example, if you're new to hiking, start with short, easy trails and work your way up to more difficult and longer treks. If you aren't sure of your footing on a tricky section of the trail, take your time to figure it out.

When going downhill, I often sit down to navigate steep sections. My pants get dirty, but I'm a lot less likely to fall or twist my ankle if I'm scooting down a rock on my butt. As much as I hike, I would never consider myself graceful or especially coordinated. In fact, when I started hiking in earnest back in college, I used to fall down almost every mountain hike. My shins, knees, and the palms of my hands were always cut up. But over time, I learned my limits. I learned that if I jumped from this rock to the next, my ankle might turn. I learned that tree roots are slippery and scree (rock debris) should be navigated with care. I also learned that the majority of falls happen when hikers are descending a mountain (rather than ascending it) because at that point, they are tired; they aren't paying as much attention; and it's more difficult to see and judge obstacles that are downhill than it is when they are uphill. So exercise caution—and bring Band-Aids and athletic tape.

If you do manage to get up and down the mountain without falling, all the power to you, but there are some other dangers that might catch you unaware. The most common mistake I see hikers make is not bringing enough water. Water is one of the most important things in your pack. How much water you need depends on the length and difficulty of the hike, but in general, if you're actively hiking, you should consume 1 liter of water every two hours, according to multiple backpacking sources.

One cool thing about Maine is that it's filled with natural water sources—crystal-clear streams and brooks that flow down mountains and feed into pristine lakes and ponds. But staying hydrated is not as simple as sticking the mouth of your water bottle in a bubbling brook. That's dangerous. Natural water sources, no matter how clean they appear, can carry bacteria and viruses that can make you very sick. The most common of these waterborne parasites is giardia, which causes an intestinal infection that results in diarrhea and dehydration. Also known as beaver fever, giardia plagues long-distance hikers that aren't vigilant about sanitizing their water.

Therefore, it's important to carry enough potable water in your backpack for the entire hike. The other option is to carry a water filtration or purification device, such as a backpacking water filter that can be worked by hand pump, a SteriPEN UV water purifier, or emergency water sterilization tablets. With one of these tools, you can filter water from streams and brooks while on the trail, resupplying with safe, fresh water when you need it.

Consider Company

Sometimes I just want to get away and enjoy the wilderness by myself. I enjoy hiking solo and do it often, so it would be hypocritical of me to chastise anyone for doing the same. However, I'd be irresponsible not to point out that it's much safer to hike with a companion or small group than it is to hike alone. And when you're with other people, you can distribute gear, which enables you to carry a greater variety of supplies, such as first aid and components of shelter. Hiking with my family and friends each year in Baxter State Park, I've experienced the benefits of having hiking buddies plenty of times. From hiking companions I've borrowed moleskin (a special bandage for blisters) and enjoyed extra water and snacks. And moving away from the practical talk, sometimes, when you're atop a mountain enjoying an unbelievable view, it's just nice to have someone to share it with.

Carry Emergency Supplies

I used to hike without a first-aid kit. Then came the day when I fell face-first on a granite ledge on Old Speck Mountain in western Maine. I was fine, but the palms of my hands and my knees were a bloody mess, and I didn't even have one Band-Aid. Luckily, I wasn't far from finishing my hike, so I simply continued down the mountain, pressing leaves on my scrapes to try to slow the bleeding. Then a group of Boy Scouts came around the bend, hiking up the mountain toward me, and I watched as their faces, one by one, expressed shock at my appearance.

"Do you need first aid?" one of the boys asked, ready to earn a badge of heroism, no doubt.

Ducking my head in embarrassment, I assured the boys I was fine and carried on down the mountain, blood streaming down my shins.

I got myself a first-aid kit pretty soon after that.

Defend Yourself

I tend to be sort of blasé when it comes to personal defense, but my family has implored me time and time again to be more vigilant in regard to protecting myself against other people and potentially dangerous wildlife, and I know they're right. It never hurts to be cautious.

In Maine, we're quite lucky not to have much in terms of dangerous wildlife. Even the big mammals we have—the moose, deer, and black bears—tend to run away upon seeing humans, especially if those humans are making a lot of noise and raising their backpacks above their heads. None of Maine's native snakes are poisonous. The only critter that poses a serious threat to a person's health is the tick, which is capable of transmitting a variety of diseases. But I address that later in another essay, so let's talk about people.

The people you meet on Maine trails are great people 99.9 percent of the time. But people with ill intentions exist, and while I think most of them tend to live and commit crimes in more populous areas, I suppose some of them might take to the woods. In fact, a handful of hikers have been killed while hiking the Appalachian Trail, the 2,180-mile hiking trail that runs from Springer Mountain in Georgia to Katahdin in Maine. It's rare, but it happens.

Self-defense—including carrying a gun—is a controversial topic. I could bow out now and say it's "up to you," but I do have a few suggestions. Pepper spray, for one, is a common and nonlethal form of defense, as is a Taser gun. But perhaps the most effective defense against dangerous people is hiking in a group rather than alone.

Make Use of Technology

I usually turn off my phone when I hike. In a lot of areas I don't have reception anyway. But the real reason I turn off my phone is because I don't want it to ring, and I don't want to answer it. It's simple. I go outside to unplug, to get away from the overload of media I experience every day through my computer, TV, radio, and phone. That being said, I've come to accept that technology can be useful outdoors. Used the right way, technology can help you minimize risks while hiking.

A GPS device is one example of helpful technology. Using this device, you can easily backtrack if you get lost or find where the nearest body of water is located. You can see how steep a slope is or find the exact summit of a mountain.

Yet the most valuable bit of technology I have for hiking safely, in my opinion, is my SPOT satellite tracker—a device that tracks me by satellite and relays my movements to a passworded website patrolled by my loved ones. The weather-resistant satellite tracker also has a function that allows me to send simple messages, including an SOS that transmits directly to local search-and-rescue teams. Sitting in a pocket in my backpack, I usually forget I even carry this nifty device. It doesn't interfere with my outdoor experience, yet it gives me peace of mind when I hike solo in remote places. I know that if things go south, someone will be able to find me.

"Expect the Best, Plan for the Worst"

As I've delved deeper into communities of outdoorsy people in Maine, I've heard several outdoor safety experts say, "Expect the best, plan for the worst, and prepare to be surprised," which is a quote by Denis Waitley, a motivational speaker, writer, and consultant from California who was actually talking about life in general, not outdoor adventures. Nevertheless, Waitley's message rings true for the outdoors crowd.

I once attended a workshop on outdoor winter survival in which the instructor went over the four necessities of survival: shelter, water, fire, and food. He then added one more: a good attitude. The ability to be positive and think rationally is extremely important in stressful outdoors situations. Without a good attitude, he said, those other necessities of survival are useless. Therefore, "expect the best." Be optimistic. Go into your adventure with confidence because you've "planned for the worst." And while the wilderness is full of surprises, you'll likely be able to handle what you come up against.

Take One Step at a Time

This past summer, while I was hiking Mount Will in Bethel, I came upon a sign that stated that 1 mile equals about 2,300 steps. And that's all hiking is—a bunch of steps. In Maine, a state with many rocks and roots, those steps aren't always so easy. Hiking in this state requires you to be present, to concentrate, and decide if a rock looks slippery or a stream is too full or fast for safe fording. Nothing else is quite as important as where your foot lands next. As I focus on stepping from one rock to the next, my everyday worries take the backburner. There's something very freeing about that.

Out on the trail, no matter how much you prepared ahead of time, you may run into challenges that you didn't expect, and you'll be forced to make decisions. So my last bit of advice is not to rush and act blindly or on a whim. If you sense a dangerous situation, slow down, assess the potential risks and rewards, then make a conscious decision. This kind of introspection costs time, but believe me, it's worth it. It can help you avoid making foolish mistakes. And in extreme cases, it can save your life.

At War with Ticks

I remember lying in the front yard of my family's home in Winterport, Maine, surrounded by dandelions, yellow blossoms as far as the eye could see. Blades of grass tickled my nose and ants crawled over my arms, making them itch. I was 9 years old or so, and what appeared to be me lazing about, enjoying the sun, was actually an act of protest. I didn't want my father to mow the lawn and kill all the flowers, I told him. Stubbornly sprawled out in the middle of our overgrown yard, I listened to him start up the lawnmower. I sat up and scowled, but honestly, I was getting bored of guarding the weeds. The sun was hot. So I hightailed it to the woods to sulk.

Back then—about 20 years ago—I didn't check myself for ticks after lying on my front lawn, even though tall grass is prime tick habitat. The tiny pests, belonging to the arachnid family, cling to the tips of grass blades as they wave their long front arms in the air, waiting for a warm-blooded creature to brush by. It's a behavior called "questing," and once a tick hitches a ride on a mouse, rabbit, deer, or human, it finds a good spot to bite. Ticks feed on blood, and in the process they can transfer a number of nasty diseases.

But I didn't know that then. It wasn't important. Back when I was 9 years old, ticks existed in Maine, but they were scarce. I could lie in the grass without fear. Today it's a different story.

To date, 14 different tick species have been found in Maine, according to the University of Maine Tick Identification Lab. Infiltrating the state from the south, these ticks carry a number of different diseases. Lyme disease, for example, is carried and transmitted by deer ticks, also known as blacklegged ticks. Early symptoms of the disease include fever, headache, fatigue, and often a skin rash that resembles a bull's-eye. Lyme disease can be detected with blood tests and treated with antibiotics. However, if untreated, the disease can spread to a person's joints and nervous system and cause serious problems, such as joint pain and swelling, facial palsy, heart palpitations, inflammation of the brain, nerve pain, and problems with short-term memory. In fact, it can be life-threatening.

Since the first case of Lyme disease was reported in Maine in 1986, the deer tick has spread throughout the entire state. Nowadays, more than 1,000 new cases of Lyme disease are reported in Maine each year.

I don't want to scare you out of the Maine woods. Ticks and the diseases they carry are a problem in many states. Connecticut, Massachusetts, New Jersey, New York, and especially Pennsylvania consistently report more new cases of Lyme disease annually than Maine. Yet people are still enjoying the outdoors. They're just doing it with some added precautions.

There are some things you can do to discourage ticks from crawling on you in the first place. Here are a few:

- Expose less skin. Wear long pants instead of shorts, and while it may not be fashionable, tuck the bottom of your pants into your socks. This greatly reduces your chances of a tick scurrying up your leg.
- Wear light-colored clothing so you can more easily see ticks and brush them off before they find your skin.
- Treat your clothing and footwear with a chemical called permethrin, which has proven effective in deterring ticks. Do not spray this on your skin.
- Use an all-natural tick repellent such as Green Mountain Tick Repellent, made in Vermont.
- Avoiding wading through grass or underbrush, which is prime tick habitat.

Yet sometimes, it seems no matter what you do, you can't keep ticks away. The most important thing you can do is to always check yourself for ticks after spending time outdoors. If you're getting into a vehicle, do a tick check before you get in. At home, shake out your clothes and put them in the washing machine. Then, because ticks are hard to drown, you'll want to put those clothes in the dryer, on high heat. But most importantly, check your whole body with your eyes and hands. Be sure to check all the nooks and crannies, where ticks love to hide. And remember that a young tick is about the size of a freckle.

Tick checks are easier to do with a partner you feel comfortable with. I once asked the assistance of my niece who was 3 years old at the time, and she teased me by pretending she found "a bug" on my back. She then let me check her for ticks. I resisted the impulse to tease her back.

It may seem like overkill, but you should check your body for ticks more than once after coming indoors. I'll never forget the time I was looking in the bathroom mirror and watched a tick crawl out of my hair and across my forehead. Ticks are good at hiding, and they're so small that they're easily overlooked.

The tick crawls around on its host and finds a spot on the skin to bite. It then burrows its mouthparts into the skin and starts sucking, filling its round body up with blood. The tick may feed for days or weeks, depending on the species of tick and its stage of life.

Is your skin crawling yet?

If you do find a tick on you, your first impulse will probably be to tear it out of your skin—but don't. It's important to remove the tick in a certain way in order to reduce your chances of contracting any illness it's carrying. There are old wives' tales about using a hot match or nail polish remover to deal with a tick. Please don't do either of those things. These methods may cause the tick to regurgitate into your bloodstream, which could transmit the disease.

What you should do is take a pair of tweezers (or a nifty little device called a tick spoon) and grasp the tick firmly as close to your skin as possible. Then slowly pull the tick away from you with steady pressure until it releases. The goal is to get the entire tick out of your skin, but if you leave some mouthparts behind, it's been found that this won't cause any further problems. Your skin will eventually push the mouthparts out.

After that's done, don't smash the tick to kill it. Its body could explode, and if the innards of a tick somehow gets into a wound on your skin, it could transmit a disease. Simply flush the tick down the toilet or put it in a baggie if you want it to be tested for disease at the nearest tick-borne disease lab. It's also a good idea to contact your doctor to talk about whether you should take antibiotics to nip any potential tick-borne disease in the bud.

Bottom line: Be aware, be informed, and be vigilant, but don't be afraid. Spending time outdoors is way too much fun to give up.

Legend

US Highway		Bench
State Road		Boat Launch
Local/County Road		Bridge
Gravel Road		Building/Point of Interest
Unpaved Road		Campground
Power Line		Campsite (backcountry)
Railroad		Gate
Trail		Parking
Bike Path		Peak/Elevation
Body of Water		Picnic Area
Marsh		Ranger Station
Sand		Restaurant
National Monument		Restroom
State Park/Preserve		Scenic View
Property Boundary		Viewing Tower
River		Visitor/Information Center
Waterfall		

Hike 1 : Rumford Whitecap Mountain in Rumford

Difficulty: Moderate to strenuous. The hike is about 5 miles out and back. Expect fairly continuous climbing with steep slopes, uneven forest floor, several brook crossings without bridges, and a rocky ridge exposed to the wind and sun atop the mountain. There is no hand-over-foot climbing, ladders, or rungs. During the spring, expect plenty of water running down sections of the trail.

Dogs: Permitted if kept under control at all times

Cost: None

Access: Day use only. Camping and fires are not permitted. The hike is easily accessible in the winter because the parking lot is plowed year-round.

Wheelchair accessibility: The trails were not constructed to be wheelchair accessible.

Hunting: Permitted in accordance with state laws

Restrooms: None

How to get there: From Rumford Center, turn right onto Andover Road. Drive 4.5 miles, then turn right onto East Andover Road. Drive about 0.2 mile to the gravel parking lot for the preserve on the left.

GPS coordinates: 44.549964, -70.684000

With a long granite ridge that tops off at 2,214 feet above sea level, Rumford White-cap Mountain offers a challenging day hike to panoramic views of the mountainous wilderness of western Maine and New Hampshire. Starting out in a quiet mixed forest, the hike is a fairly continuous climb, crossing several tumbling brooks on the way to the mountain's open summit.

Much of Rumford Whitecap is located on Mahoosuc Land Trust's 752-acre Rumford Whitecap Mountain Preserve, where two blazed hiking trails lead to its top. The Red-Orange Trail, marked with red and orange blazes, starts across the road from the preserve parking lot by the red gate. The Starr Trail, marked with yellow, starts across the road from the parking lot by the gray gate (northwest of the Red-Orange Trail). Both trails climb the mountain, starting out gradually and becoming steeper. To lessen the degree of the slope, trail builders have constructed the trails so they switchback (zigzag) up the steepest slopes.

After about 2 miles, the two trails come together about 0.5 mile before the summit. From that point on, the trail is marked with red and orange blazes. It officially ends at the summit, which is marked by a small round metal geological survey marker embedded in the bedrock. Blink and you might miss it.

Past the summit, you'll notice red marks on the rock and trees that closely resemble the trail markers. This red paint is marking the preserve boundary. Do not follow them.

Whether you hike up and down the Red-Orange Trail or Starr Trail, or create a loop of the two, the hike is approximately 5 miles total. Also of note, the Red-Orange Trail intersects with what's known as the Black-White Trail 1.63 miles from

Rumford Whitecap Mountain in Rumford

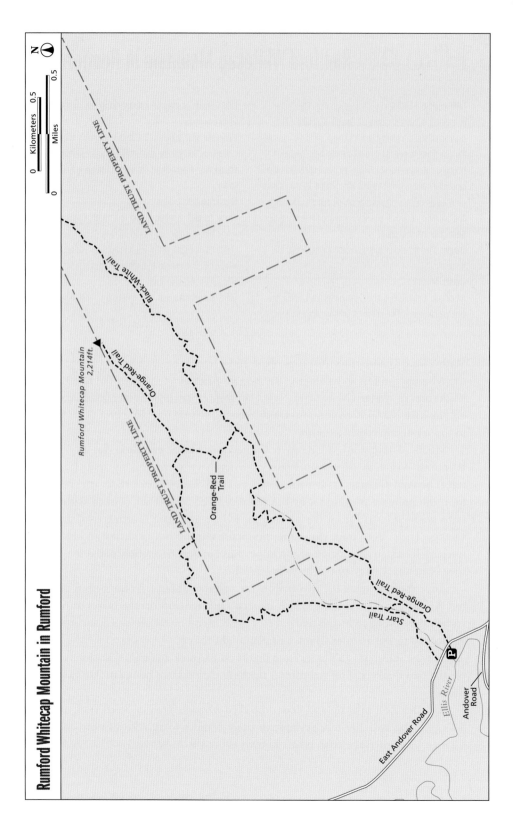

Rumford Whitecap Mountain
2,214ft.

LAND TRUST PROPERTY LINE

LAND TRUST PROPERTY LINE

Black-White Trail

Orange-Red Trail

Orange-Red Trail

Orange-Red Trail

Starr Trail

East Andover Road

Ellis River

Andover Road

N

Kilometers 0   0.5

Miles 0   0.5

The sun sinks behind the Appalachian Mountains in February, as seen from the top of Rumford Whitecap Mountain.

the trailhead. The Black-White Trail is 4.75 miles and travels east to Black Mountain, another great hike.

The mixed forest covering the slopes of Rumford Whitecap Mountain includes a wide variety of tree species, including large white and yellow birch trees, stands of striped maple (which is also known as moose maple or moosewood, since it's a favorite snack for moose), tall hemlocks, and red pines. In fact, the mountain is home to what's thought to be the largest red pine woodland in the state, covering 210 acres. This red pine woodland is located on the lower portion of the mountain's exposed ridge, mostly above 1,700 feet elevation, on the western half of the mountain.

Rumford Whitecap is also home to a rare natural community known as a "mid-elevation bald," characterized by patchy subalpine to alpine vegetation and dominated by low mats of black crowberry, alpine bilberry, sheep laurel, and lowbush blueberry broken up by patches of lichen-covered bedrock. This rare community is located on the higher, more exposed areas on the east end of the ridge of Rumford Whitecap and covers about 55 acres.

Also of note, two rare plant species—silverling and smooth sandwort (both of which produce small white flowers)—have been documented along the mountain's ridge.

Rumford Whitecap Mountain Preserve was established in 2007, when the Mahoosuc Land Trust acquired the property with the help of more than 500 donors, as well as grants from Land for Maine's Future and five charitable foundations. It's especially important to stay on trail during your hike because large portions of the trails are on private property. Also, staying on trail will help you avoid trampling rare and delicate alpine plants.

For more information: Visit www.mahoosuc.org or call (207) 824-3806.

Personal note: It had been an eventful February weekend. I'd kicked it off with nighttime cusk fishing on a frozen lake, something I'd never done before. The next day, I learned how to ride a snowmobile, something I was admittedly nervous about, and I brushed up on my map and compass knowledge. I'd learned tricks on starting a fire in the snow and cooked a gourmet meal—with the help of many other women—over that fire. The Becoming an Outdoors Woman in Maine Winter Skills Weekend had been a blast, but I was nearly spent. And on Sunday, after all that excitement, I'm not sure what possessed me to drive to the trailhead of Rumford Whitecap Mountain.

When I arrived at the icy parking area, I didn't really feel like snowshoeing for hours. I smelled like campfire smoke, and I'd stayed up late the night before, fly tying, of all things. But I felt it would be a huge opportunity missed if I returned home

Water flows down the mountain on the Red-Orange Trail in February.

A sign marks the intersection of the Red-Orange Trail and Black-White Trail.

without visiting a mountain in western Maine. Sometimes you just have to suck it up. So that's what I did. I threw on an extra wool shirt, slipped snow baskets onto my new LEKI trekking poles, stuffed an extra hat and jacket into my pack, checked the batteries in my satellite tracker, consulted the trail map, crossed the road, climbed over the snowbank, fastened my snowshoes, and hit the trail.

Lucky for me, the deep snow on the Red-Orange Trail had been packed down by snowmobilers and snowshoers that had come before me, making it easy to snowshoe on. Eventually the trail branched off from the snowmobile trail and became narrower, but still fairly wide and easy to follow. When the mountainside became steeper, I snapped up my snowshoes' heel lifts, which are little metal bars that pop up under my heels that give me support as I climb, taking some of the strain off my calves. They helped quite a bit.

Despite it being in the 20s that day, recent warm weather had water pouring down the mountain, often along the trail. Icicles had formed in the most interesting shapes along the edges of the flowing water, which spilled over rocks in tiny waterfalls and churned into foam that then froze, crumbling to the touch of my mitten.

As I neared the top of the mountain and the red pines started to disappear, I was greeted by a bitter wind that nearly knocked me off balance. Its ferocity worried me as I struggled forward, my snowshoes clacking and screeching over patches of ice and granite. The wind had swept the ridge clean of snow in many areas, but I didn't want to struggle with the straps of my snowshoes in such bitter cold, so I just kept them strapped to my feet, zipped up my windproof fleece jacket, swapped my beanie for a warmer fur-lined bomber hat, and carried on toward the summit.

Snow coats the exposed bedrock near the top of Rumford Whitecap Mountain in February.

It wasn't long before I reached a granite hump that appeared to be the summit, where I knelt down to inspect a geological survey marker. My cheeks burning and eyes watering from the cold, I remained there just long enough to take video and photos of the stunning view. To the east rose nearby Black Mountain and a line of wind turbines forming a trail to the north, and to the west—where the sun was rapidly sinking—the Appalachian Mountains. Facing the sun, I descended the mountain as quickly as my legs would carry me and made it to the parking area before dark.

Hike 2: Aziscohos Mountain in Lincoln Plantation

Difficulty: Strenuous due to the steep, rocky stretch of trail near the top of the mountain. The 2-mile trail starts out easy, though a bit muddy in the spring and early summer, then becomes increasingly difficult as it climbs the mountain. Water runs over the trail in many areas. Watch out for slippery roots and rocks.
Dogs: Permitted if kept under control at all times
Cost: None
Access: The trailhead is on a major road, making this hike easily accessible year-round. The trail is suitable for foot traffic only.
Wheelchair accessibility: The trails were not constructed to be wheelchair accessible.

Hunting: Only with private landowner permission
Restrooms: None
How to get there: From Oquossoc, start at the intersection of Route 17 and Route 16 at the center of town. Drive west on Route 16 for 17.9 miles. The trailhead will be on your left, just before a gravel drive. The trail used to be marked with a sign, but in June 2016 the sign was missing and the trail was marked with two red blazes, painted on trees on either side of the trail. If you reach Aziscohos Dam, you've driven exactly 1 mile too far.
GPS coordinates: 44.933457, -70.986470

Rising 3,215 feet above sea level in western Maine, Aziscohos Mountain has attracted hikers since the 1800s because of the panoramic view of the area's mountains, lakes, and ponds offered at its bald summit.

The name *Aziscohos* is believed to be derived from a word in the Algonquian languages spoken by the native peoples of Maine. However, the meaning of the name is debated. Some sources state that *Aziscohos* is an Abenaki word meaning "small pine trees," while other sources state it is likely derived from a similar Penobscot word meaning "covered with mud." Having hiked Aziscohos on a rainy day in June, I can confirm that I saw plenty of both—pine trees and mud—on the mountain.

Furthermore, many sources offer a different spelling for the mountain—Aziscoos. In fact, this spelling is used in an article about the mountain's history, laminated and posted at the trail intersection near the summit of the mountain.

Today Aziscohos Mountain is located on privately owned property, but hikers continue to climb to its summit using two trails. Those who attempt to hike the mountain do so at their own risk. Though located on a well-traveled road, the trail is fairly remote. There is no trail register and no one checking in on the trail on a regular basis. Also, cell phone service is extremely limited on the mountain.

The 2-mile Aziscohos Mountain Trail starts on Route 16, exactly 1 mile east of Aziscohos Dam, and is currently maintained by the Trails for Rangeley Area Coalition, a local group that maintains a handful of hiking trails in the Rangeley Lakes area. The trail is marked with red blazes and starts out fairly easy, traveling through a hardwood forest and up a gentle slope. As is the case with many mountain trails, the trail becomes increasingly steep and rocky as it nears the summit. Just below the

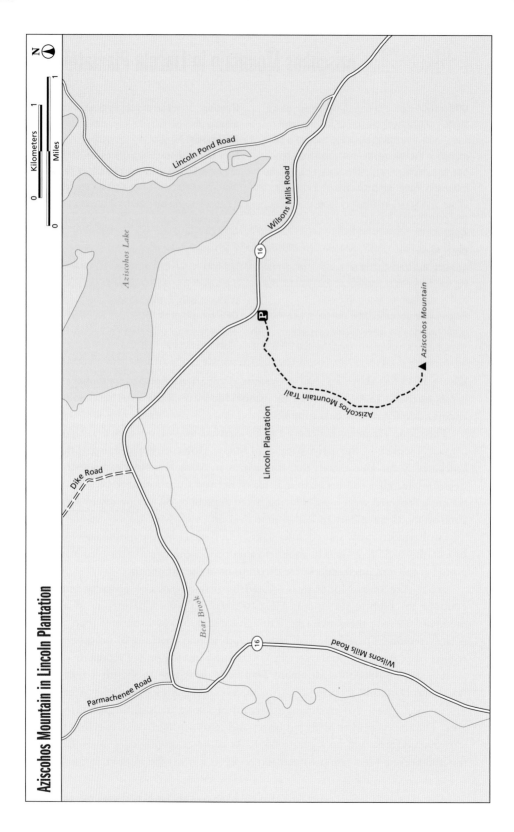

Aziscohos Mountain in Lincoln Plantation

The Aziscohos Mountain Trail is marked with red blazes and maintained by the Trails for Rangeley Area Coalition.

summit, in a sheltered area, the trail intersects with the Tower Man's Trail. At this intersection, veer left to hike the remaining 0.1 mile to the summit, which is marked with a wooden sign nestled in stunted evergreens.

There is no sign at the trailhead, but a short distance into the forest, a sign reading Aziscohos Mountain is posted on a tree, and beneath it, a smaller sign that says RT 3.4, indicating the hike is 3.4 miles round-trip. However, a sign near the top of the mountain contradicts this, indicating that the trail is 2 miles long, so up and back would be 4 miles. In the Appalachian Mountain Club's *Maine Mountain Guide,* 10th edition, Carey Kish confirms that the trail is indeed 2 miles.

The other trail, the Tower Man's Trail, is 2.4 miles long, according to an old sign at the intersection near the top of the mountain. It has not been maintained in recent years, but locals sometimes use it. Its trailhead is also on Route 16, close to the Aziscohos Dam.

Atop Aziscohos Mountain, hikers are rewarded with a view of the surrounding mountains, lakes, and ponds of western Maine and nearby New Hampshire. Major landmarks include the long, narrow Aziscohos Lake to the north and a chain of mountains to the west that include Half Moon Mountain, Diamond Peaks, and Mount Dustan.

Because of the open view atop Aziscohos Mountain, a fire lookout tower was erected on its summit in 1910, according to the Forest Fire Lookout Association Maine Chapter, then rebuilt three times, in 1917, 1919, and 1929. Information posted

A sign marks the summit, which on a clear day offers a panoramic view of the many mountains and lakes of western Maine and New Hampshire.

near the mountain's summit states that Basil Melvin was the mountain's last watchman in 1968. Thus abandoned, the tower collapsed by the mid-1980s, and the majority of the ruined tower was removed from the mountain in 2004, according to the Forest Fire Lookout Association. However, the concrete base of the tower still remains.

For more information: Call the Trails for Rangeley Area Coalition at (207) 864-3951.

Personal note: On a bit of a whim, I booked a cozy 1950s cabin in Rangeley in early June so I could spend a few days exploring trails in western Maine. Accompanied by my husband, Derek, and our dog, Oreo, we spent three days checking out a variety of trails, from easy bird walks to rugged mountain trails. And though the sun refused to shine all weekend, we had a good time outdoors, enjoying lupine fields and waterfalls in the rain.

Aziscohos Mountain—a hike I read about on Mainetrailfinder.com and in the AMC's *Maine Mountain Guide*—was the last outing of our trip. I had heard that the mountain offered some of the finest views in the state, but when we hiked it on Sunday, the summit was socked in with clouds. Bracing myself against a cold, wet wind, I photographed the summit sign, then retreated to the sheltered trail intersection

The trail is rocky and crossed with slippery tree roots near the top of the mountain.

before the summit, where I stubbornly stood in the rain for 40 minutes, waiting for the clouds to clear.

"They're not going anywhere," Derek said.

"Do a sun dance," I suggested, watching the dreary sky overhead.

"Look at Oreo," he said, pointing to our dog. He was shivering. My resolve crumbled, and with a nod of my head, we headed back down the mountain.

Though we weren't rewarded with sweeping views at the summit, we still had an enjoyable hike. The forest at the base of the mountain was a sea of bright green leaves, the muddy trail lined with ferns and the white blossoms of bunchberry and foam flowers. Farther up the mountain's slope, we stopped to look at mushrooms and tiny ice-filled caves, formed in the spaces between large slabs of granite.

The hike was also a physical challenge. The steep slope, combined with slippery, wet granite and tree roots, required us to pay attention to our footing and help each other from time to time. The experience led me to dream about even taller mountains, greater challenges, and sunnier days.

Hike 3: Mount Will in Bethel

Difficulty: Moderate to strenuous. The loop trail on Mount Will is about 3 miles long and climbs to the top of the mountain, which rises about 1,700 feet above sea level. Challenges you'll experience on this trail include steep slopes, masses of tangled tree roots, and long stretches of steady climbing.

Dogs: Permitted if kept under control at all times

Cost: None

Access: The trail is for foot traffic only. The parking lot is plowed by the town in the winter.

Wheelchair accessibility: The trails were not constructed to be wheelchair accessible.

Hunting: Only with private landowner permission

Restrooms: None

How to get there: Starting at Riverside State Rest Area off Route 2 in Bethel, drive 1.9 miles east (technically north) on Route 2 (also known as Mayville Road) to the gravel parking area for the Mount Will Trail, which is on the left, directly across the road from the transfer and recycling station. The trail starts at the parking area by a kiosk that displays a detailed trail map and a list of rules for trail users.

GPS coordinates: 44.478248, -70.796168

Rising just over 1,700 feet above sea level in the western Maine town of Bethel, Mount Will offers a moderately challenging loop hike to ledges with spectacular views of the Androscoggin River Valley and western Maine mountains. The 3-mile trail on the mountain was initially built by the Bethel Conservation Commission to increase public awareness of the natural resources and beauty of the river valley. Then, in 2013, the trail was rebuilt with assistance from Mahoosuc Pathways and Oxford County Conservation Corps.

From the trail parking area, the Mount Will Trail enters the woods and climbs gradually through a mixed forest. The trail is marked with blue blazes and is well maintained, making it easy to follow. In less than 0.1 mile, the trail splits into a loop that can be hiked in either direction.

If you veer left, hiking the loop clockwise, you'll climb steadily up the mountain to reach the South Cliffs in a little under a mile. Located about 1,450 feet above sea level, the South Cliffs offer open views of the Androscoggin Valley and Bethel village. Total elevation gain from the trailhead to this point is about 730 feet.

Throughout the hike you'll come across a number of interpretive signs that were created by students of Telstar Freshman Academy in Bryant Pond under the guidance of Mahoosuc Pathways' executive director, Gabe Perkins, in 2016 and 2017. The signs offer interesting facts about nature seen on the hike. For example, did you know that Maine produces 90 percent of the wild blueberries grown in North America?

From the South Cliffs, the trail continues 1.2 miles to the North Ledges. This section of the trail climbs to a point near the mountain's wooded summit, which is 1,704 feet above sea level, then descends to the North Ledges, which are about 1,350 feet above sea level and provide a different view of Androscoggin Valley. The summit of

Mount Will in Bethel

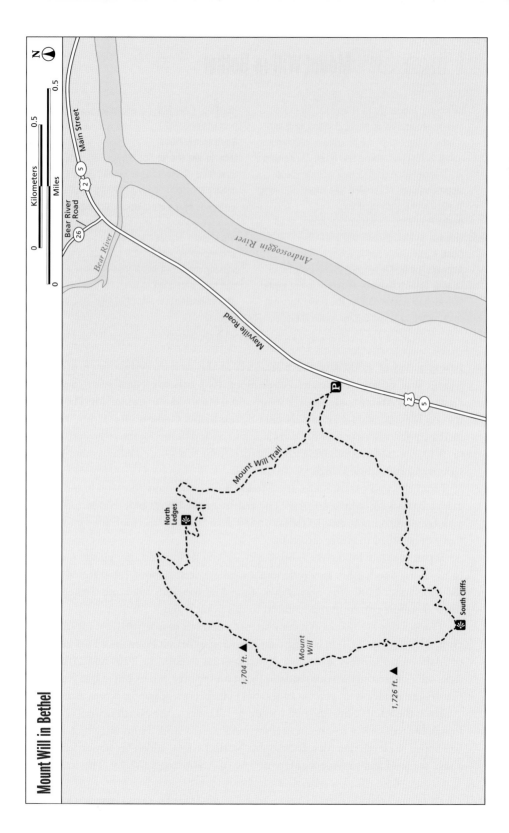

Outlooks on Mount Will offer great views of the farms and forestland of western Maine.

the mountain is not marked with a sign; however, a large cairn has been constructed on the trail near the summit.

While hiking on the trail between the South Cliffs and North Ledges, you'll come to a grassy woods road marked with a sign that reads Gray Memorial. If you leave the blazed trail and follow the old road a short distance uphill to a mossy clearing, you'll come to the memorial, a plaque placed in a stone in memory of Leroy W. Gray II and Brenda Mae Gray, who died in an airplane crash at the site on September 25, 1992.

From the North Ledges, it's about 0.9 mile down the mountain to the trailhead. In the steepest sections, the trail switchbacks (zigzags) so the slope of the trail isn't too drastic.

Some of the hiking trail that explores Mount Will is located within the 115-acre Bethel Town Forest, but the majority of the trail is on private land with landowner permission. The trail is maintained by the town in collaboration with Mahoosuc Pathways, Inc., whose mission is to develop, maintain, and promote multiuse recreational trails in the Mahoosuc region.

For more information: Call the Bethel Town Office at (207) 824-2669 or visit www.bethelmaine.com; or call Mahoosuc Pathways at (207) 200-8240 or visit www .mahoosucpathways.org.

Derek hikes up a steep, root-covered slope on the trail that explores Mount Will.

Personal note: I first hiked Mount Will in 2014, while traveling in western Maine to interview the organizers of the first-ever Tough Mountain Challenge held at Sunday River. The well-known ski resort was about two and a half hours from my home, so I woke with the sun that day and hit the road early so I could fit in the hike up Mount Will before the interviews I'd scheduled for the afternoon.

I saw five other hikers on Mount Will that day—two couples and a dog—but for the most part, I was kept company by chattering red squirrels and chipmunks. The trail glittered with mica, a fairly common mineral found in the bedrock of western Maine. Resembling glass, mica forms in thin sheets that can easily be flaked off and crumbled into tiny shards. When I was a young girl, I thought it looked an awful lot like fairy dust. In addition to being rather pretty, mica is heat-resistant and it doesn't conduct electricity. Therefore, sheets of the mineral are used as electrical and thermal insulators and as windows in stoves and kerosene heaters.

Mica is one of the many beautiful minerals you can find in western Maine, a hot spot for mining gemstones such as tourmalines, garnets, rubies, and byrls, as well as mica and feldspar. I learned about the area's many hidden treasures while writing a story about recreational mining—mining for gemstones as a fun activity or hobby—for the BDN. For the story, I interviewed Zoltan and Jody Matolcsy, owners of Maine Mineral Adventures, and talked with them about their experiences searching for gems in the area. I learned, for example, that just a 30-minute drive from Mount Will is Mount Mica, the location of the oldest tourmaline mine in North America. I also learned that Maine's gems are usually found in pegmatite, a coarse granite that

Left: A poisonous mushroom and an acorn make an interesting duo beside the Mount Will Trail in August.
Right: A giant patch of jewelweed is in bloom in August beside the trail. Jewelweed is a natural remedy for the itchy oils of poison ivy, poison oak, and stinging nettle, all of which grow in Maine.

contains pockets or voids where gems find the right condition to grow. A band of pegmatite runs through central and western Maine, drawing geologists and gemologists from all over the world.

I returned to Mount Will with my husband, Derek, and our dog, Oreo, in the summer of 2017 to record any changes in the mountain's loop trail for this guidebook. The only significant change I noticed was that the trail was easier to follow, with better signage and freshly painted blazes. The trail had settled into the landscape, worn into the forest floor by the boots of local residents, no doubt. Signs marked the trail at each of its 3 miles, even giving the approximate number of steps you would have taken by each point (with 3 miles equaling about 6,900 steps).

As we hiked to the South Cliffs that day, we came across a giant patch of jewelweed, a leafy plant with bright orange blossoms and pods of seeds that burst at the touch. I used to love playing with these plants as a child, and let's be honest, I still do. As I photographed the sea of orange blossoms, I told Derek that I heard jewelweed can be used to treat poison ivy. Coincidentally, a few hundred feet farther on the trail, we came to an interpretive sign affirming my claim. Jewelweed can also be used to neutralize the itch-inducing oils of poison oak and stinging nettle, according to the display.

Also during the hike, I stopped to photograph spindle-shaped yellow coral mushrooms, a cluster of orange chicken mushrooms, and a pale assembly of turkey tail

Derek and Oreo hike through a beautiful forest on Mount Will.

mushrooms growing on a tree stump. At the North Ledges, we picked a few lowbush blueberries to snack on, just for fun, then descended the mountain on a fairly gradual slope. We only spotted one other hiker that day, despite it being a sunny Saturday in August, so I think it's safe to say this mountain isn't at all a crowded one.

Hike 4: Wells Barrens Preserve in Wells

Difficulty: Easy to moderate. The 3.6 miles of trails on the preserve are wide and fairly smooth and travel over even terrain, surfaced with gravel or mowed grass and shrubs. One challenge you may face is overgrown trails, especially the White Trail. The most well-maintained trail is the Loop Trail, which starts and ends at the driveway near the Nature Conservancy office and leads to all the other trails in the network.

Dogs: Not permitted

Cost: None

Access: The preserve is open from dawn until dusk. Bikes, fires, and camping are prohibited. Snowmobiles are allowed on an authorized trail on the property, but ATVs and other motorized vehicles are not permitted.

Wheelchair accessibility: The trails were not constructed to be wheelchair accessible.

Hunting: Not permitted

Restrooms: None

How to get there: Take I-95 exit 19 to Wells. At the light, turn right (west) onto Route 109 and drive about 5 miles toward Sanford. Turn right onto Wire Road and drive about 1.5 miles; the parking lot will be on your left. Park outside the gated driveway that leads into the preserve and is for authorized vehicles only. Walk into the preserve on the driveway and the Loop Trail will soon start on your right, marked with a large sign.

GPS coordinates: 43.375638, -70.648438

The sandy, shrubby landscape of Wells Barrens Preserve, punctuated with twisted pitch pines and bright wood lilies, is a place of beauty and ecological importance. Home to a number of rare plants and birds, the preserve was established in 2007, when the Nature Conservancy purchased 367 acres from Wells Blueberry Inc. Today the public can explore this property on foot, on a network of trails that form four interconnecting loops and altogether total 3.6 miles.

Each trail is blazed with a different color. Starting at the parking area, visitors must walk past the gate and into the preserve on a short driveway. Just before reaching the large white building that serves as an office for the Nature Conservancy, the Yellow Trail begins on your right, marked with a sign that says Loop Trail. Just beyond that sign is an educational display about black racer snakes.

The Yellow Trail forms the main loop trail on the property, measuring 1.5 miles long. Branching off of this main loop is the 0.5-mile Red Trail, 0.5-mile Blue Trail, and 1.1-mile White Trail, all of which loop back to the Yellow Trail. Because the trail network travels through sandplain grasslands and barrens, there is little shelter from the elements. Wear sunscreen and sunglasses.

Wells Barrens, together with the adjacent Kennebunk Plains, is the largest intact example of sandplain grasslands remaining in New England. It was formed by melting glaciers about 14,000 years ago, when meltwater streams deposited sand and gravel over the land, according to a report by Beginning with Habitat, a collaborative conservation program of federal, state, and local agencies and nongovernmental

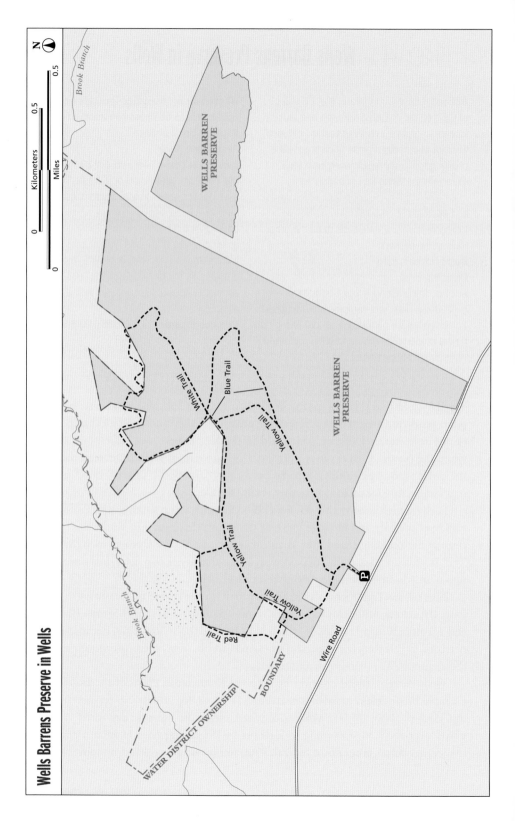

Wells Barrens Preserve in Wells

The bright blossoms of wood lilies stand out against the greenery of the sandplain grasslands in Wells Barrens Preserve in mid-July.

organizations. This type of soil has little capacity to hold water and nutrients, meaning all plants and animals living on it need to be adapted to frequent droughts and fires.

According to the report, the area is home to four natural community types—sandplain grassland, pitch pine–scrub oak barrens, pitch pine–heath barrens, and red maple alluvial swamp forest—and supports populations of 14 rare plant and animal species.

The grasslands on the property are home to what may be the world's largest population of northern blazing star, a tall perennial with showy, thistle-like flowers that are a light purple. Other rare plants on the property include toothed white-topped aster and upright bindweed.

The site is also one of the few known locations in Maine that the nonpoisonous black racer snake calls home. Though common in the South, the black racer snake is on Maine's endangered species list. It is also Maine's largest snake, growing up to 6 feet long, and is known for being especially fast, according to the Maine Department of Inland Fisheries and Wildlife. As its name implies, the snake is uniformly black or bluish black, with shiny scales and a white chin and throat.

Wells Barrens and the Kennebunk Plains are also home to the ribbon snake and wood turtle, two reptiles that are listed as species of special concern in Maine. Bird species found here include (but are certainly not limited to) grasshopper sparrows, sandpipers, vesper sparrows, and eastern meadowlarks.

The Wells Barrens Preserve features sandplain grassland and early successional forest that has ecological importance as critical wildlife habitat.

If you are particularly interested in the geology of the land, be sure to check out the preserve's Red Trail, which has a side trail leading out to a sand pit that is just outside the preserve boundary but is owned by the water district. The preserve lies above an important aquifer within the Branch Brook Watershed, a key drinking water resource for Kennebunk, Kennebunkport, and Wells.

For more information: Call the Nature Conservancy Maine field office at (207) 729-5181 or visit www.nature.org.

Personal note: It was a gloomy July afternoon when I first set foot on Wells Barrens Preserve. Starting my adventures on the Yellow Trail, I was soon in awe of the abundance of blueberries peppering the landscape, ripe and shining with beads of rain. Dark clouds lingered overhead, but it appeared the showers had passed.

A white-tailed deer darted across the trail ahead of me. Crows made strange sounds from the forest nearby, and a gentle wind kept the mosquitoes at bay. I scanned the shrubs and grasses for the rare black racer snake. Every once in awhile, a dark, rain-soaked root of a pitch pine tree would trick me into thinking I'd finally stumbled upon the snake, but it wasn't in the cards that day. And quite honestly, I knew my odds of finding the endangered snake were fairly low, so I wasn't too disappointed.

As I walked the trails, I paused several times to photograph plants, including bright wood lilies, which are a neon color that is neither orange, pink, nor red, but something in between. Songbirds flitted through the bushes, moving too quickly for me to even hope to identify them. I kept spotting one bird in particular over and over again. It flew into a bush, making the leaves tremble as it hopped from branch to branch. In the fading daylight, I could tell the bird was rather large, with a dark back and head, a long dark tail, and a white and reddish-orange breast. My first two thoughts, American robin and evening grosbeak, I knew were incorrect because of the pattern on the bird's chest. So I photographed the bird and later looked it up online using the Cornell Lab of Ornithology website. It appeared to be an eastern towhee, and to be sure, I compared sound clips from my hike to sound clips of the towhee's call online. They matched perfectly.

Before wrapping up my adventure, I hiked part of the White Trail, which was a bit overgrown, and the entire Red Trail so I could visit the sand pit that I noticed on the trail map posted on the kiosk at the parking area. Branching off the Red Trail, a tiny side trail led to the sand pit, where I wandered, inspecting deer and wild turkey tracks and sifting the fine sand through my fingers. Caught up in my own thoughts, I lost track of where I'd entered the sand pit. "I'm lost in the desert," I thought, then

An educational display about the black racer snake, a species that is listed as endangered in Maine, is located near the beginning of the Loop Trail. This rare snake has been found on the preserve.

Blueberries grow in abundance in the sandplain grasslands of Wells Barrens Preserve.

laughed at my own joke. Tracing the edge of the pit, I eventually found the trail and ducked back into the woods to retrace my steps to the trail network.

Hike 5: Spear Farm Estuary Preserve in Yarmouth

Difficulty: Easy. The preserve is home to about 2 miles of intersecting trails that travel over a fairly smooth forest floor with some exposed tree roots and small hills.

Dogs: Permitted if kept on leash when within 300 feet of any trailhead. Farther from the trailheads, dogs must be either on leash or under voice control.

Cost: None

Access: The trail is for foot traffic only (including snowshoeing and cross-country skiing) from dawn until dusk, year-round. Bicycles are not permitted. The pond is open for skating in the winter. The use of metal detectors is allowed only by permit. Nighttime use can be granted with special permission acquired through the Yarmouth Town Office. Fires and motorized vehicles are not permitted.

Wheelchair accessibility: The trails were not constructed to be wheelchair accessible.

Hunting: Not permitted

Restrooms: None

How to get there: The address of the preserve parking area is 445 Bayview St. in Yarmouth. To get there from Route 1 in Yarmouth, turn onto Route 88 (Spring Street) near Cumberland Farms and drive 0.2 mile, then turn left onto Bayview Street and drive 0.9 mile. The parking area for the preserve will be on your right.

GPS coordinates: 43.796348, -70.158345

Located in the most populous county in Maine, Spear Farm Estuary Preserve is a quiet getaway that offers many opportunities for viewing wildlife. The 55.5-acre preserve is on a tidal section of the Royal River and includes upland forest, a tiny field, a small apple orchard, picnic areas, seasonal streams, marshlands, and a freshwater pond constructed in 1968 by the US Fish and Wildlife Service as a way to improve wading bird and waterfowl habitat in the area. These habitats can be explored by a simple network of intersecting footpaths that total about 2 miles altogether.

Owned and managed by the town of Yarmouth, the preserve is protected through a conservation easement held by the Royal River Conservation Trust. Originally known as Bayview Estuary Preserve, it was conserved in phases between 2004 and 2011 through a combination of federal, state, local, and private funds, as well as gifts of land. Its name was changed to Spear Farm Estuary Preserve in honor of the Spear family, which donated 13 acres to the project in 2005.

The preserve trail network starts at a parking area and barn off Bayview Street, with a trail leading across a 1-acre field to enter the woods. This small field is dominated by barnyard grasses, goldenrod, tall white aster, and cinquefoil, according to a management plan for the preserve created by the Town of Yarmouth Parks & Land Committee in 2012.

Historically the property was farmed, primarily for hay, in the late 1800s and early 1900s. It was also home to cattle and was harvested for timber. Today about two-thirds of the preserve is forested uplands. The forest stands range from hardwood (red oak, black cherry, and sugar, red, and Norway maples) to thickets of white pine. The forests are also home to a number of shrubby invasive plants

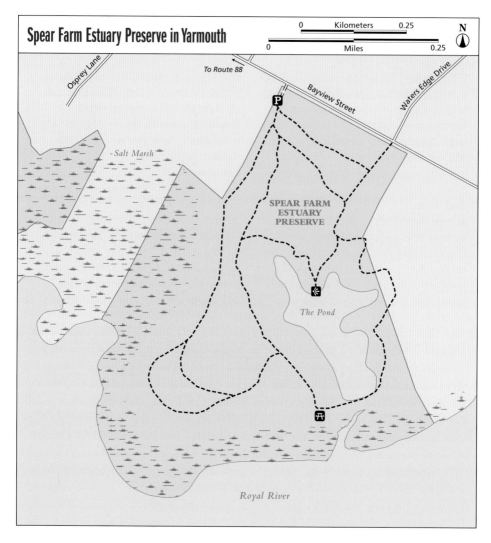

Osprey Lane

To Route 88

Bayview Street

Waters Edge Drive

P

- Salt Marsh

SPEAR FARM
ESTUARY
PRESERVE

The Pond

Royal River

including smooth buckthorn, Morrow's honeysuckle, Japanese barberry, and Asiatic bittersweet.

The intersecting trails that make up the network are fairly smooth and travel over gentle hills. The trails also include long spans of bog bridging, as well as benches and picnic areas at nice rest spots.

Five educational displays located throughout the network offer information about the environment. For example, one display focuses on the freshwater marsh and the different species it attracts, including bullfrogs and belted kingfishers. Other wildlife often spotted on the property include white-tailed deer, gray and red squirrels, red foxes, wild turkeys, snowy egrets, great blue herons, black-crowned night herons, wood ducks, black ducks, bald eagles, ospreys, and a variety of songbirds. Good birding sites on the property are in the oak and pine stands, along the bluffs, the salt marsh

The Royal River as seen from an outlook on the trail network of Spear Farm Estuary Preserve in August

edge, on the earthen dam, and the northern end of the freshwater pond, according to the Royal River Land Trust.

Pockets of forested and non-forested wetlands can be found around the pond. A small apple orchard is located south of the pond, a picnic area is near the northwest side of the pond, and a new apple orchard was planted in the summer of 2011 in the far eastern corner of the preserve. The pond is fringed with meadowsweet, winterberry, alder, and in the wetter areas, pickerelweed, cattails, cinnamon fern, and native swamp loosestrife. The forested wetlands are dominated by red maple, white ash, interrupted fern, lady fern, and wood fern; and the salt marsh contains a mix of salt marsh hay, black rush, and salt marsh grasses, according to the management plan.

The pink blossoms of ornamental jewelweed stand out in the greenery along the trail.

For more information: Visit www.rrct.org or call (207) 847-9399.

Personal note: As I walked between the pond and the marshes lining the Royal River in late August, a black and orange butterfly fluttered across the path and into the jumble of black-eyed Susans, goldenrod, red clover, and Queen Anne's lace. I crept closer to the butterfly as it fed on the nectar of select blossoms, only to be nearly struck in the nose by another butterfly as it fluttered past. Both were monarchs, a butterfly that migrates from its wintering grounds in Mexico each year to lay its eggs on Maine milkweed. Once quite common in the state, the monarch's numbers have declined dramatically in recent years, and biologists believe it's for a number of reasons, including the use of pesticides across the United States and deforestation of their wintering grounds in Mexico. In Maine, people have been planting more milkweed and other plants that monarchs need, hoping that by providing these habitats, this beautiful pollinator might bounce back.

The monarchs that migrate to Maine have a fascinating life cycle. Starting in Mexico, they fly about 2,300 miles to Maine, stopping off along the way to refuel their tiny bodies on the nectar of various plants. These monarchs then find milkweed in Maine, lay eggs, and die. The eggs hatch into caterpillars, which can only eat milkweed, and these caterpillars grow until they undergo metamorphosis by creating a cocoon—something nearly all Maine schoolchildren learn about at some

A group of snowy egrets hunt for food in Spear Farm Estuary Preserve's man-made pond.

A smooth trail winds through the forest of Spear Farm Estuary Preserve.

point or another. From the cocoon the butterfly emerges, then the whole cycle starts over again, typically three times within a Maine summer. It's that third generation that then migrates down to Mexico. How they know where to go is a mystery, and biologists have determined that the third generation is actually built a bit differently than the ones that follow it. It's specifically designed to be able to migrate that long distance, twice. In Mexico it will winter, then migrate back to Maine, which means that particular generation lives much longer than the two generations that precede it.

As I stared at the monarchs feeding off the wildflowers at Spear Farm Estuary Preserve in late August, I wondered what generation they belonged to. Would they live a short life, laying eggs of the third generation and dying before winter? Or were they of that third generation, built to fly across the country and return the following year?

Continuing on my way, I came to an educational display by the marsh that named some of the wading birds often seen on the property, including the snowy egret. Then, just a few minutes later, as I walked along the perimeter of the pond, I spotted a group of large white birds fishing along the water's edge. Following a trail around the pond, I drew closer and used my 100-300mm camera lens to zoom in on the birds and determine that they were indeed snowy egrets. Some of them were fairly young, betrayed by their long legs being a pale greenish color rather than black, which they become as they mature. Their big feet, however, always remain bright yellow. These snow-white birds moved slowly, wading through the shallows or walking along a dead tree that had fallen into the pond. And when they spotted their quarry, they darted their head forward, straightening their long necks and snatching up an insect, fish, or frog with their sharp black beak.

Hike 6: Devil's Back Trail Area in Harpswell

Difficulty: Easy to moderate. Altogether the trails in the network total 2.2 miles and form two long loops with cutoff trails that allow for shorter hikes. For the most part, the trails travel over uneven terrain with plenty of exposed tree roots and rocks. The trails also travel over small but steep hills and a few narrow sections along the edge of steep slopes.

Dogs: Permitted if kept under control at all times

Cost: None

Access: Campfires, camping, and overnight parking are not permitted. The trail is for foot traffic only and is open year-round.

Wheelchair accessibility: The trails were not constructed to be wheelchair accessible.

Hunting: Not permitted

Restrooms: None

How to get there: From Cooks Corner in Bruns-wick—which is the intersection of Route 24 (Gurnet Road) and Route 248 (Bath Road)—drive south on Route 24 for 9.4 miles. Soon after crossing onto Orr's Island, the parking lot will be on your left. The trailhead for the east trail network is located at the corner of the parking lot; the trailhead for the west trail network is directly across the road.

GPS coordinates: 43.786564, -69.949193

Located just north of Portland on the Maine coast, the town of Harpswell is made up of a peninsula and more than 30 islands. One of these islands is Orr's Island, which is connected to the mainland by a short causeway and is home to the recently developed Devil's Back Trail Area.

Named after the ridge that runs down the center of the island's narrow northern tip, the Devil's Back Trail Area is composed of two loop trails, one on each side of Route 24, which runs down the "spine" of Devil's Back. Owned and managed by the town of Harpswell, the west side of the trail network opened in 2012 and the east side opened in 2016. While still not widely known, it is becoming a popular place for local residents and summer visitors to enjoy the island's mossy old forest and rugged coastline. Altogether the trails total 2.2 miles, with the west loop trail being slightly larger than the east loop trail, according to the trail map provided on the town website.

On the west side of the road, the trail system explores a mixed forest that includes clusters of ferns, old abandoned apple trees, a stand of large cedars, and towering red pines. The trail starts out wide and smooth, gently descending the Devil's Back and splitting into a long skinny loop that is bridged with three cutoff trails. A long section of the loop follows the shore of Long Cove, where in places the bedrock slopes into the ocean to be covered by rockweed and waves. Across the water is West Harpswell, and in the cove you'll likely see a number of boats mingling with sea ducks and gulls. Ospreys are also commonly seen fishing offshore.

As the trail gets farther from the trailhead, it becomes more narrow and challenging as it navigates small hills. In fact, one section of the trail travels up along the side of such a steep hill that the town has strung up a rope between trees as a sort of

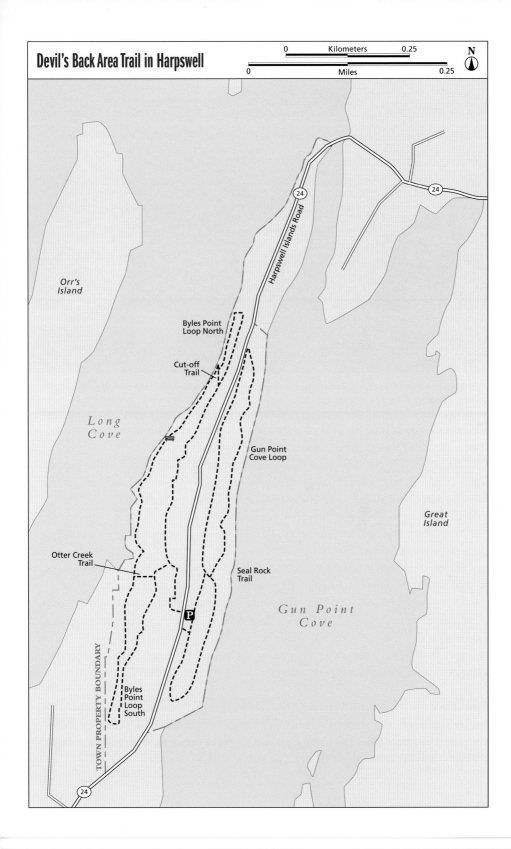

Devil's Back Area Trail in Harpswell

Orr's Island

Long Cove

Byles Point Loop North

Cut-off Trail

Gun Point Cove Loop

Otter Creek Trail

Seal Rock Trail

Great Island

Gun Point Cove

TOWN PROPERTY BOUNDARY

Byles Point Loop South

Harpswell Islands Road

24

24

A granite bench is located at a scenic viewpoint of Long Cove on the west loop trail of the Devil's Back Trail Area in Harpswell.

handrail to assist hikers. But as a whole, these trails—the trails on the west side of the road—are a bit easier than the trails on the east side of the road.

The trail on the east side of the road also forms a long loop, bisected with a cutoff trail. It passes through a forest made up of a wide variety of softwood and hardwood trees, with dramatic slopes that lead down to small cliffs along Gun Point Cove. From various viewpoints along the shore, hikers can observe Seal Rock, where seals often rest in the sun. And across the water is Great Island—just another part of the oddly shaped town of Harpswell.

The trails on both sides of the road are marked with white, blue, and yellow paint, with the different colors assigned to different trails to make navigation easier. Visitor guidelines are posted online and on a tree near the beginning of the east trail network.

Though the trails of the Devil's Back Trail Area are new, the conservation of the land happened long ago. The town acquired the land—approximately 36 acres—in two parcels in 1946. That early conservation of the land accounts for the number of large trees you see on the property today.

For more information: Visit the Town of Harpswell website at www.harpswell .maine.gov or call the town office at (207) 833-5771. The trail is also featured on the Harpswell Heritage Land Trust website at https://hhltmaine.org, where you can find a wealth of information about many other public trails in the area.

Personal note: My first experience of the Devil's Back Trail Area was in the summer of 2013, just after the opening of the west loop and long before the opening of the east loop. My sister, Jillian, and I—along with my dog, Oreo—hiked the west loop as part of the Harpswell Hiking Challenge, in which we hiked eight trails totaling about 10 miles in one day (though most participants complete the challenge in two or more days).

I remember it being particularly hot and humid that day, but we managed to complete the challenge, though it took us from early morning until sundown. In our haste, we were unable to notice the small details of each trail we hiked, but the challenge gave us an overall idea of just how many awesome trails exist in Harpswell for the public to enjoy, thanks to the town recreation department and the local Harpswell Heritage Land Trust.

What I remembered of Devil's Back from that challenge was the preserve's beautiful mossy forest, as well as the hilly, rocky terrain. Four years later, hearing that the trail area had expanded, I resolved to return for a slower, more thoughtful hike. On a Sunday in early July, my husband, Derek, and I—along with Oreo—arrived at the

Derek and Oreo navigate a steep section of trail while hiking in the Devil's Back Trail Area.

A dead horseshoe crab in the mud and grass on the shore of Long Cove

new Devil's Back parking lot to find at least four other vehicles already parked, and as we set out along the east loop, we came across some of the cars' owners.

A salty ocean breeze flowed through the forest, keeping away the mosquitoes, and sunlight glittered off the water, which was a striking blue-green color that Derek and I debated over—was it aqua or turquoise or teal?

After completing that loop, we crossed the road to walk the west loop. Cutting across the loop to the water on the Otter Creek Trail, we found a beach-like area where we let Oreo wade into the shallow water and splash about. Unfortunately, he drank a good amount of saltwater and became dehydrated and sick for the next couple of days. In fact, I was so concerned about him that I stayed home from work and watched over him like a mother hen while feeding him wet dog food mixed with Pedialyte. The treatment worked, but it doesn't in all cases. My friend recently had to take both of her dogs to the vet for the same issue, and they had to be rehydrated with IVs.

Anyway—Oreo is fine, and while he splashed about in Long Cove, I found a dead horseshoe crab in the grass along the shore. It was a lucky find, seeing how horseshoe crabs live most of their lives in the deep ocean, only traveling ashore to mate during very specific times. I've written about these rather ancient creatures before, and the more I learn, the more fascinating they become. With a shell shaped like a horseshoe, these animals have a clear lineage stretching back more than 400 million years, before the dinosaurs.

By the time we finished our thorough exploration of the trail area, it was time to head home, cook dinner, and prepare for the work week, feeling refreshed from a day of sun and sea breeze.

◀ *Derek and Oreo walk along the shore of Long Cove.*

Hike 7: Swan Island in the Kennebec River

Difficulty: Easy to moderate. The island features 7 miles of hiking trails, as well as a 4.5-mile dirt road that is great for walking or biking. The road, which runs from one end of Swan Island to the other, is the easiest way to explore the island. The hiking trails are well marked and maintained and travel over unimproved forest floor and mowed edges of fields.

Dogs: Not permitted

Cost: Day use is $8 per person and can be paid to iron rangers (metal containers) located at boat launches on the island. Children 5 years old and younger are free. The campsites, which include a fire pit and lean-to and can fit up to 6 people, are $20 a night. Canoe and kayak rentals are $10 an hour or $35 a day, and firewood is $4 a bundle. Season passes are also available.

Access: The island is only accessible by boat and is open to the public from the beginning of May through Oct. During that time, you can access the island by paddling your own kayak or canoe across the Kennebec River to one of the island's public landings or you can reserve a spot on a passenger-only ferry, which leaves Richmond at 9:15 a.m., 11:15 a.m., 1:15 p.m., and 3:15 p.m. each day and must be reserved ahead of time by calling (207) 547-5322. The ferry does not accept vehicles (it's too small), but bicycles are welcome. The ferry ride lasts about 5 minutes and is followed by an optional shuttle by truck to the island campground. Paddling from the Richmond boat launch to the campground boat launch (which is on the opposite side of the island) takes about 30 minutes.

Wheelchair accessibility: The island roads and trails were not designed to be wheelchair accessible; however, the old gravel road that runs from one end of the island to the other is wide and fairly smooth.

Hunting: Not permitted

Restrooms: A building at the campground features flush toilets, sinks, and drinking water.

How to get there: Getting to Swan Island requires a 5-minute ferry ride (which must be reserved ahead of time) across the Kennebec River. People also paddle to the island in canoe or kayak. To get to the ferry landing, take I-295 to exit 43 (Richmond-Litchfield), then follow Route 197 east for about 3 miles to Richmond Village. At the intersection of Route 197 and Route 24, turn left; the Swan Island Ferry parking lot will immediately be on your right, marked with a large sign.

After ferrying across the river, island visitors can get into the bed of a shuttle pickup truck, which has cushioned benches, for a slow 1.6-mile ride to the campground. At the campground is a public boat launch and a kiosk displaying a trail map. The hiking trails start at the campground.

GPS coordinates: Richmond boat launch parking area, 44.087912, -69.798422

Located in the Kennebec River, between the towns of Richmond and Dresden, Swan Island was once home to a small community. Today the 2,019-acre island is a state-owned wildlife management area that is an excellent spot for hiking, camping, and wildlife watching. It's also a place where you can walk back in time. With remains of the abandoned town described through educational displays, it's easy to imagine what life would have been like on the island in the 1800s.

A 4.5-mile gravel road runs through the center of the island from north to south, from the ferry launch to Theobald Point. Along the way, it passes a campground and

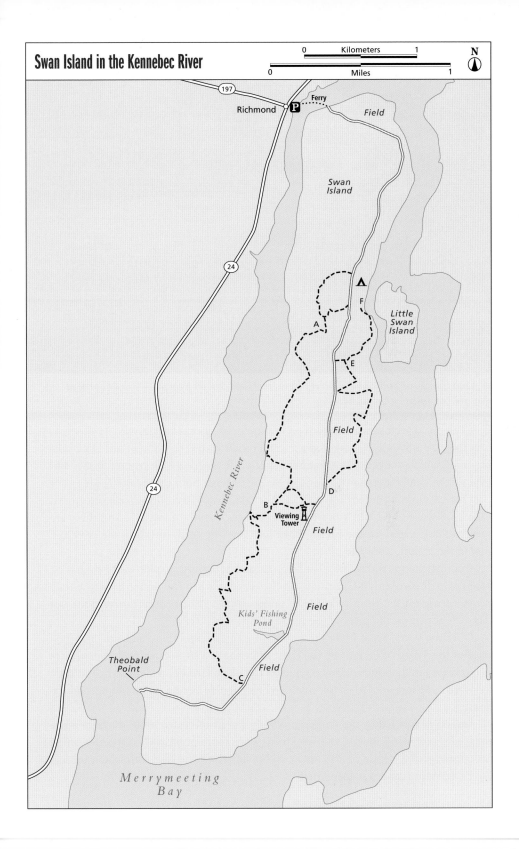

A granite bench sits at the edge of a field on Swan Island, not far from the 4.5-mile dirt road that runs the length of the island.

boat launch, as well as five abandoned homes, fields, a cemetery, a wildlife observation tower, a kids-only fishing pond, and trailheads to several hiking trails. The hiking trails, which altogether total about 7 miles, are marked with painted blazes and explore the wilder areas of the island, traveling through both forests and fields.

Once a summer destination for the Abenaki, Swan Island may have once been called *Swango,* an Abenaki word that translates to "islands of eagles." And there are plenty of bald eagles on the island. They soar over the fields to fish in the river and nest in the island's tall white pines.

Another theory is that the island was named by English explorers for migrating swans. The first record of Caucasians on the island was in 1730, and in 1750 the only people living on the island was the Whidden family. A fascinating story about this family is posted on the gates of the island's Curtis Cemetery.

Over the years, Swan Island evolved into a small community and was incorporated as the Town of Perkins in 1847. By 1860, the town's population hit its peak at 100 residents in 27 homes. Many people on the island farmed, evidenced by the large fields that still remain. Other jobs included fishing, lumbering, shipbuilding, and ice cutting.

Several factors led to the community's decline in the early 1900s. Refrigeration reduced the demand for ice, and steel boats were more popular than wooden ships. Wood was getting scarce on the island, and pollution of the river eliminated fishing. By 1936, Swan Island was abandoned.

The Maine Department of Inland Fisheries and Wildlife (DIF&W) began acquiring properties on the island as early as the 1940s, but it wasn't until 1988 that the entire island—and nearby Little Swan Island—was under state ownership. It officially became the Steve Powell Wildlife Management Area, named in memory of one of the first biologists working and living on the island after it became a state wildlife management area.

Five historic homes on the island remain standing today, including the house Powell lived in with his family in the 1940s. These houses, each located along the island's one gravel road, can be viewed from the outside, where educational displays offer visitors fascinating tidbits of history.

For wildlife enthusiasts, Swan Island is an especially great place for birding because it's home to so many different habitats. Bird nesting boxes dot the island's old fields—where bobolinks, tree swallows, and eastern phoebes are common—and the island's ponds, wetlands, mixed forest, and 536 acres of freshwater tidal flats draw many other species. In fact, a long checklist of the island's bird species is available on the DIF&W website, which also includes a butterfly checklist and self-guided tour brochure.

A white-tailed deer pauses at the edge of a field in June on Swan Island.

One of the most frequently spotted mammals on the island is white-tailed deer, but there are other, more elusive creatures such as coyotes, foxes, porcupines, raccoons, and sometimes moose, according to the DIF&W. One of the best ways to spot these animals is by spending some time in the island's wildlife observation tower—which was originally a fire tower built on Frye Mountain in Montville in 1931. The tower is located between two fields that contain food plots and nesting boxes, about 1.5 miles south of the campground if walking on the road.

The campground, located in a grassy field overlooking the Kennebec River, is composed of 10 Adirondack shelters (lean-tos), each with a fire pit and picnic table, as well as a group site. These campsites are spaced around the edges of the field, which is kept mowed, and nearby is a building that includes modern restrooms, a sink for washing dishes, and drinking water. The campground also features a boat launch, dock, and a boathouse that serves as a classroom, store, and a place to gather island brochures.

For more information: Call (207) 547-5322 or visit www.maine.gov/swanisland.

Lacey climbs to the top of a wildlife observation tower that's open to the public.

A bald eagle perches in a stand of birches on the shore of Little Swan Island, and can easily be seen from the campground on Swan Island.

Personal note: "There are bones in there," said my friend Lacey as she looked through the empty window frame of the abandoned machine shop.

"No way," I said, hurrying over to her.

We'd been joking about how some people say Swan Island is haunted. To us, the island's abandoned buildings had character. Their peeling paint and overgrown gardens spoke of days gone by, of living people—not ghosts. Yet here we were, staring at a large pile of a bones. Of course, on closer inspection, they were deer bones. The skull, complete with small antlers, was easy to identify.

Moving to the side of the old machine shop, we found a door that was broken nearly in half, leaving a sizable hole for critters to invade the building. The pile of bones was just inside, and a trail of bones—including an interesting piece of the deer's spine—littered the yard outside. We tried to piece together what had happened and could only arrive at coyotes, the island's top predator, having created the scene somehow.

Lacey and I had traveled to the island earlier that day on the ferry, pitched a tent at our reserved campsite, and gathered firewood. We then hit the trails on the east side of the island, finding a beautiful sea of ferns and a rocky perch on the river's edge, before emerging onto the island road across from the old Curtis Cemetery.

On that Saturday in early June, we were two of several campers on the island. We'd taken the ferry over with a couple and a group of women throwing an out-doorsy bachelorette party. They'd blindfolded the bride-to-be and canoed her across the river ahead of the ferry, and some of them took the ferry, bringing the bulk of their supplies. Lacey and I watched from across the campground field as they decorated their lean-to with streamers. But to our surprise, we didn't hear any hooting or hollering that evening as we sat by our campfire. The women were clearly being considerate of other campers. We fell asleep to the chirp of frogs from the nearby beaver pond.

The next morning, we woke early, forced out of the tent by the heat of the sun. The weather report called for temperatures climbing to 90 degrees Fahrenheit, and it had been correct. As I munched on a granola bar and apple, I wandered around the campground with my camera, photographing an eastern phoebe flying to and from its nest, which was tucked into the rafters of our lean-to and contained three perfect white eggs (we checked). Then, across the water, Lacey spotted two bald eagles, and I managed to photograph one as it perched on a tree limb, watching the water for fish.

That morning, we took a long walk in the sun, first to view a beaver lodge and wetland, then back down the island road all the way to Theobald Point. The trek brought our total trip walking distance to about 11 miles. Along the way we spotted at least five white-tailed deer, four wild turkeys, several bald eagles, and a furry

A well and old outbuilding stand outside the abandoned Robinson-Powell House on Swan Island.

A tree swallow perches in the sun. The bird is using one of the island's many nesting boxes.

creature that looked a lot like a bobcat as it dashed across the road in front of us. I introduced Lacey to the robotic call of the bobolink and the loud voice of the bullfrog. And Lacey, who owns a gardening business, pointed out many plants, including the fragrant honeysuckle bushes near our campsite and the sweet fern and giant rosebushes lining the road.

"I bet it's even more beautiful later in the summer, when the roses bloom," Lacey said at one point.

I agreed, though it was hard to imagine the place more lovely. The Elysian Fields—the heavenly resting place for the souls of heroes in Greek mythology—came to mind as I looked out over fields dotted with yellow buttercups and Indian paintbrushes. Maybe we'll just have to return and see if she's right. I imagine with all the island's giant oaks and sugar maples, it's a gorgeous spot in the fall as well.

Hike 8:   Round Top Mountain in Rome

Difficulty: Moderate. The loop hike, including the spur trail to the summit, is 4.7 miles total. The trail includes especially rocky sections and areas of steady climbing, broken up by easy, level stretches of trail.

Dogs: Permitted if kept on leash

Cost: None

Access: The Round Top Mountain Trail is for foot traffic only, but a part of the hike runs along a section of the multiuse Kennebec Highlands Trail, which is used by snowmobilers, mountain bikers, cross-country skiers, and horseback riders. The trails are open from dawn until dusk year-round. In the winter, the parking area is plowed.

Wheelchair accessibility: The trails were not constructed to be wheelchair accessible.

Hunting: Permitted; however, firearms cannot be discharged within 300 feet of campsites, marked hiking trails, and boat launches, and loaded firearms are not permitted in campsites.

Restrooms: None

How to get there: From Route 27 in Rome, turn onto Watson Pond Road and drive about 4 miles. The large gravel trailhead parking lot is on your right, just before Wildflower Estates.

GPS coordinates: 44.530195, -69.922529

Rising 1,133 feet above sea level, Round Top Mountain is the highest peak in the Kennebec Highlands, a group of hills and mountains in central Maine. The 4.7-mile hike of the mountain travels mostly through a deciduous forest, past giant boulders to rocky ledges that offer stunning views of the area. The trail also visits the summit of the mountain, which is marked with a sign and offers a partial view of the region over the treetops.

Starting at a parking lot off Watson Pond Road, the Round Top Mountain Trail begins with a gradual rocky climb through a mostly deciduous forest. A short way into the forest is a registration kiosk, where hikers are asked to fill out a form. Beyond the kiosk, the blue-blazed trail continues to climb gradually, passing through a stand of hemlocks, where you'll cross over an old rock wall. The trail then heads gradually downhill to cross a trickling brook and meet a major trail intersection at the 1-mile mark.

At the intersection, the Round Top Mountain Trail splits into a loop. It also intersects the South Vienna Mountain Trail and the Kennebec Highlands Trail. Signs mark this intersection to help you select your route. If you head straight, hiking the loop clockwise, you'll hike gradually up the south slope of the mountain to meet the spur trail that leads to the summit in 0.8 mile. If instead you turn right at the intersection, hiking the loop counterclockwise, it's 1.3 miles to the spur trail. Hiking that way, you'll follow the wide multiuse Kennebec Highlands Trail for a short, relatively flat stretch. You'll then turn left, leaving the Kennebec Highlands Trail behind to hike rather steeply up the eastern slope of the mountain. Just before reaching the spur trail, you'll come to outcroppings that provide the most-open views you'll find

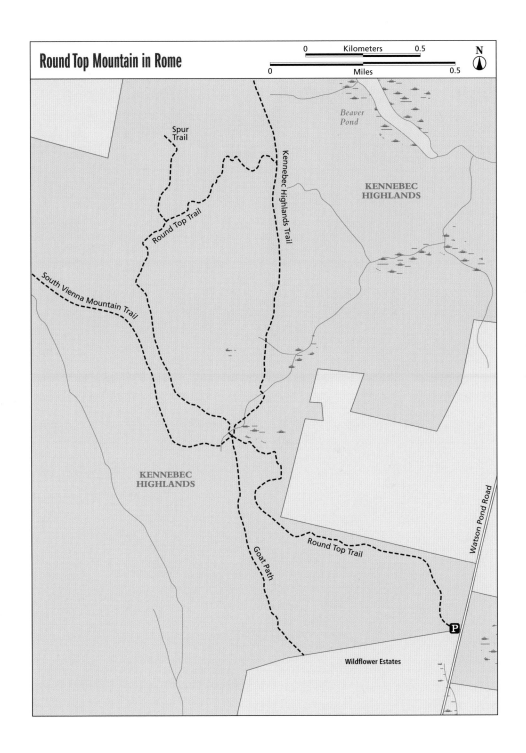

Round Top Mountain in Rome

0 Kilometers 0.5

0 Miles 0.5

N

Beaver Pond

Spur Trail

Kennebec Highlands Trail

KENNEBEC HIGHLANDS

Round Top Trail

South Vienna Mountain Trail

KENNEBEC HIGHLANDS

Round Top Trail

Goat Path

Watson Pond Road

P

Wildflower Estates

on the hike. From patches of open bedrock you can look to the east to Great Pond and Long Pond.

The entire trail is located within the 6,800-acre Kennebec Highlands Public Reserved Land, which is the largest contiguous block of conserved land in central Maine and contains the highest peaks in Kennebec County, as well as miles of pristine streams, a variety of wetlands, and five undeveloped ponds. The conservation of this property, which lies just north of Augusta, began in 1998, when the Belgrade Regional Conservation Alliance (BRCA) initiated the project and raised funds to purchase the land, with the assistance of grants from the Land for Maine's Future program. The BRCA is now working with the Maine Department of Agriculture, Conservation, and Forestry to make the land more accessible to the public for traditional outdoor activities such as hiking, hunting, and fishing.

The organization's long-term goal is to protect even more land in the area, expanding the Kennebec Highlands to 11,000 acres. According to the BRCA website, this goal is based on the minimum habitat requirements for certain wildlife species in the area, including interior nesting birds, raptors such as owls, and wide-ranging species such as bear, bobcat, moose, lynx, and otter.

For more information: Visit www.belgradelakes.org, call (207) 495-6039, or visit the BRCA office at 137 Main St. in Belgrade, open 8 a.m. to 5 p.m. Mon through Fri.

Personal note: Just before snowstorm Nemo hit Maine with high winds and heavy snowfall in February 2013, I decided it'd be a good time to hike Round Top Mountain—and bring along a family member. My cousin Eve Jordan, for some reason, agreed.

Soon after leaving the trailhead, we realized the trail was too icy to navigate without ice cleats. Fortunately, I had brought along two pairs of ice cleats (though still in the vehicle), Christmas presents I had yet to test out. Eve and I returned to the parking area, strapped the cleats tightly to our boots, and set off on the trail with a new confidence, knowing we could tackle any slippery surface. Our new footgear clacked over ice and rocks dusted with fresh snow.

As we hiked through snow flurries under a white sky, we counted five woodpeckers (hairy and downy) and saw evidence of porcupines—teeth marks on trees stripped of bark. We wrapped scarves around our faces to shield them from the biting cold, with the temperature hovering around 10 degrees Fahrenheit. The highest point of the hike, which is located on the Spur Trail, was close to the summit, but we did not find a summit sign anywhere on the trail network. The trail did pass several outlooks, though the views of nearby mountains and ponds were mostly obscured by clouds and snow that day.

A stone staircase curves around a large boulder on the Round Top Mountain Trail.

A viewpoint on the Round Top Mountain Trail provides a partial view of the Belgrade Lakes in September.

When I returned to Round Top Mountain in September of 2017, the leaves were beginning to turn red and orange. Clouds drifted lazily across the sky, blocking the late summer sun for long periods of time as I trudged through the forest under a thick, leafy canopy with my husband, Derek; my mother-in-law, Geneva; and my dog, Oreo.

I've heard that spring and fall are the best times to hunt for wild mushrooms, and that seemed to ring true that day. A few large mushrooms snagged our attention early on in the hike, and from that point on, we were scanning the ground and tree trunks for different varieties, even though we seldom knew the mushrooms' names, let alone whether they were edible, poisonous, medicinal, or hallucinogenic. They were interesting to look at, nevertheless, and that's what I do for the most part when I'm in nature—look, not touch. On white birch trees we found bulbous white mushrooms, and in the leaf litter we found mushrooms with purple gills under their caps. On an old stump we found chunky orange mushrooms that may have been the edible fungus known as chicken of the woods, and standing solitary beside the trail was a tall white mushroom, which may very well have been the fatally poisonous mushroom known by many names, including destroying angel.

Atop the mountain, as we sat on a patch of bare bedrock and ate PB&J sandwiches, we discussed the difference between hornets, wasps, bumblebees, honey bees, and yellow jackets as we watched a variety of the stinging insects buzz around us, gathering nectar from goldenrod and other late-summer blossoms. We then headed

The poisonous mushroom called destroying angel stands out on the mossy forest floor on Round Top Mountain.

back down the spur trail and continued clockwise on the loop to the more-open outlooks of the region. Looking out over the forest, I spied maple leaves turning red here and there, as well as the bright red berries of mountain ash. Two turkey vultures circled high above the forest in the distance, riding thermals by catching the rising air with their big dark wings. We took in the scene for a few minutes, then continued down the trail, enjoying the rich scents of the forest, the slowly decaying leaves, and the sprouting mushrooms.

Hike 9: Annie Sturgis Sanctuary in Vassalboro

Difficulty: Easy to moderate. Altogether the trails in the network total roughly 2 miles. The trails and all intersections are marked with blazes and signs. Expect small hills, a few rocky sections, and exposed tree roots.

Dogs: Not permitted

Cost: None

Access: The sanctuary is open daily Apr through Oct from dawn to dusk. The trails are for foot traffic only. Camping, picnicking, fires, smoking, bikes, ATVs, and snowmobiles are not permitted on the property.

Wheelchair accessibility: The trails were not constructed to be wheelchair accessible.

Hunting: Not permitted

Restrooms: None

How to get there: Take I-95 to exit 113 (Augusta/Belfast), then go east on Route 3 for 1.7 miles, crossing the Kennebec River. Just after crossing the river, at the intersection of Route 201 and Route 102, turn left onto Route 201 and drive north for about 4.1 miles. Turn left onto Cushnoc Road (in the town of Vassalboro) and drive approximately 1.5 miles; the sanctuary trailhead will be on your left, on the west side of the road. Park on the shoulder of the road, well out of the way of traffic and without blocking any nearby driveways.

GPS coordinates: 44.403258, -69.709498

An excellent place to find woodland flowers and wildlife, the 40-acre Annie Sturgis Sanctuary in Vassalboro features a simple, 2-mile trail network that is open to foot traffic only. Owned and maintained by the New England Wild Flower Society, this property is home to what's known as the largest stand of wild ginger in Maine, as well as a variety of wildflowers, including bloodroot, trout lily, and purple trillium.

A simple wooden sign, located at the edge of Cushnoc Road, marks the trailhead for the sanctuary. This sign includes the name of the sanctuary in red, as well as a small, framed trail map. From the sign, a wide trail follows a line of tall pines between two lawns, then enters the forest. Stay on the right side of the pine trees, as the trail map instructs, and respect the privacy of the nearby landowners. In the forest, the trail eventually splits into a big loop, with a spur trail and a smaller loop at its northeast end.

Signs are located at trail intersections, and they can help you decide what route to take. Some signs note the mileage of the trail ahead, while others indicate the most prominent features on the trail. For example, at the first trail intersection, a sign indicates that you should turn right for the best wildflower trails.

At a trail intersection farther into the network, a sign points left to Mount Tom and right to the Ginger Trail, a 0.75-mile loop trail where you can find the wild ginger, as well as some nice scenery along a winding brook. The short trail up Mount Tom is wide and smooth, gradually climbing to the top of the hill, where the trail dead-ends at the picturesque remains of an old chimney and fireplace constructed out of local stones and bricks. Also atop Mount Tom is a wooden bench that was a gift

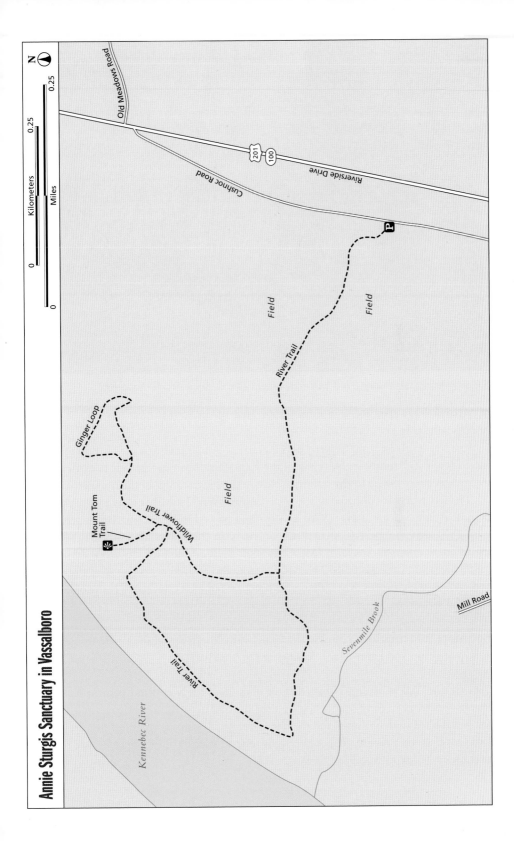

Annie Sturgis Sanctuary in Vassalboro

An old chimney stands atop a hill known as Mount Tom in Annie Sturgis Sanctuary.

of Marilyn J. Dwelley, the steward who directed the crew that built the sanctuary's bridges and trails.

Last but not least is the River Loop Return, a 1-mile trail that travels through a mixed forest and comes within view of the Kennebec River as it travels back to the trail intersection closest to the trailhead, closing the biggest loop in the trail network.

The sanctuary was donated to the New England Wild Flower Society by the children of Annie Sturgis (1883–1973) in 1987 and named in her honor. But it wasn't until 1991 that the society opened the sanctuary to the public after working with the Maine Conservation Corps (MCC) to clear trails on the property along former bridle paths and carriage trails. The MCC teams also built four bridges over streams and ravines, which today have fallen into disrepair but aren't necessary for people to cross the waterways.

For more information: Visit www.newenglandwild.org or call the sanctuary stewards, Gail Brum and Lynn-Marie Kikutis, at (207) 623-9340.

Personal note: Yellow trumpet-shaped trout lilies lined the woodland path in Annie Sturgis Sanctuary in early May, when I visited the trail network for the first time. The forest was filled with birdsong, and the trees were just beginning to unfurl new leaves. I was visiting the property at just the right time to capture the unique beauty of a landscape filled with woodland flowers.

In addition to the hundreds of yellow lilies that had sprouted from the forest floor, purple trillium were in bloom, a woodland flower with three deep-red petals. In juxtaposition to their beauty, the trillium is said to have the smell of rotting meat, and therefore also bears the common name "stinking Benjamin."

Bloodroot was also in bloom throughout the forest that day, though I didn't know the flower by sight and had to look it up later. Growing low to the ground, this white woodland flower reminded me of a daisy, with eight long, rounded petals and a yellow center. While later identifying the flower online, I learned that bloodroot derives its common name from the fact that it has reddish roots that produce bright orange sap. The plant has a long history of being used for medicinal purposes, but with care. Bloodroot produces a toxin, stored in its roots, and this toxin kills living cells. It has been used to treat everything from warts to rheumatism, but an overdose of bloodroot extract can cause vomiting and loss of consciousness.

I suppose I could take credit for my impeccable timing, but I had no idea so many flowers would be in bloom so early in the year. I'm a botanical newbie, and I'd simply been lucky.

Purple trillium is in bloom in the woods of Annie Sturgis Sanctuary in May.

Trout lilies bloom in many places along the trails.

Bloodroot is in bloom in the Annie Sturgis Sanctuary woods.

While photographing trout lilies, I noticed a tiny jumping spider crawling across a dead oak leaf. Most spiders give me goosebumps, but jumping spiders are oddly adorable. Two of their eight eyes are exceptionally large and located right at the front of their head, reminding me of a person wearing thick-lensed glasses that magnify their eyes in a comical fashion. I'm not the only one who finds jumping spiders to be cute.

A tiny jumping spider walks across a dead oak leaf at Annie Sturgis Sanctuary.

I belong to a few insect photography groups on Facebook, and the jumping spider photos are always popular.

As I moved from field to forest, I walked through a noisy group of white-throated sparrows and black-capped chickadees. A few minutes later, I spied a hairy wood-pecker drilling on a tree, and I'm sure there were plenty of birds nearby that I didn't see. As I walked the entire trail network, up and down Mount Tom, then around the Ginger Trail, birds talked to me the whole way. I heard and saw a lot in the forest that day, but crazily enough, I missed the famous patch of wild ginger. Though I had some idea of what it would look like, I must have passed by it. Maybe I'll return someday to see if I can find it.

Hike 10: Spruce Mountain in Rockport

Difficulty: Moderate. The 2.5-mile trail that explores Spruce Mountain travels over hilly, rocky terrain and features long stretches of climbing that is neither gradual nor particularly steep. The distance of the hike can be anywhere from 0.8 mile to 3.8 miles, depending on which of the two trailheads you start at and how many outlooks atop the mountain you want to visit.

Dogs: Permitted if kept on leash

Cost: None

Access: The trail is for foot traffic only. During the winter, if the snowbanks aren't too high, you can still park to the side of Mount Pleasant Street to hike from the west trailhead. The parking lot at the east trailhead on Route 17 is sporadically plowed throughout the winter.

Wheelchair accessibility: The trails were not constructed to be wheelchair accessible.

Hunting: Only with private landowner permission

Restrooms: None

How to get there: To reach the Route 17 trailhead, start at the intersection of Route 17 and Route 90 in West Rockport and drive 1.8 miles north on Route 17; the parking area will be on your right, marked with a large wooden sign. To hike toward Spruce Mountain, cross the road and hike south on the Georges Highland Path.

To reach the Mount Pleasant Street trailhead from Route 17 in Hope, turn onto Harts Mill Road and drive 0.3 mile, then turn left onto Fogler Road and drive 0.6 mile. Turn left onto Mount Pleasant Street and drive about 1 mile to the vehicle turnout on your left. Or, from Route 17 in Rockport, it's about 2.4 miles on Mount Pleasant Street to this turnout. The trail starts there, marked with a GHP sign. Hike east on the trail, passing under power lines and crossing a clearing before entering the forest. (Do not cross the road and hike the trail west or you'll be hiking Pleasant Mountain.)

GPS coordinates: Mount Pleasant Street trailhead, 44.194351, -69.181893; Route 17 trailhead, 44.201724, -69.158945

Rising 955 feet above sea level, Spruce Mountain is one of the many small peaks in Midcoast Maine that offer great views of the region. As a hiking destination, it's often overlooked due to its slightly taller neighbors, Ragged Mountain and Bald Rock Mountain, which are both excellent hikes but can get a bit crowded in the summertime. Featuring a 2.5-mile hiking trail, Spruce Mountain is covered with a forest composed mostly of various deciduous trees (ironically, given its name), but on its ridge are three outlooks that offer open views of the region, as well as a few spruce trees.

Spanning from Mount Pleasant Street and Route 17 in Rockport, the 2.5-mile trail that travels up and over Spruce Mountain is a part of the much longer Georges Highland Path, a 50-mile network of blue-blazed footpaths in Midcoast Maine built and maintained by the Georges River Land Trust. Because the trail travels up and over the mountain, there are two options for hiking to the mountain's summit. The east trailhead is located on Mount Pleasant Street, and the west trailhead is on Route 17.

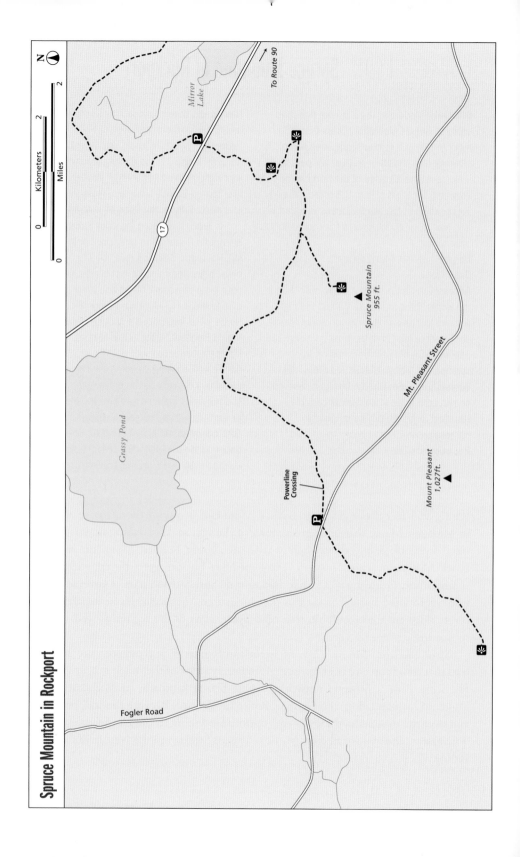

Spruce Mountain in Rockport

Mirror Lake

To Route 90

Kilometers

Miles

N

17

Grassy Pond

Spruce Mountain
955 ft.

Mt. Pleasant Street

Powerline
Crossing

Mount Pleasant
1,027ft.

Fogler Road

Mirror Lake as seen from an outlook on Spruce Mountain in October

I suggest starting at Mount Pleasant if you want a longer trek with more seclusion. From the turnout, the trail descends into a grassy area where it crosses under power lines and then enters the forest to travel steeply downhill before leveling off somewhat. In a forest filled with oak, maple, and beech trees, the trail navigates several hills and threads through boulders as it approaches the mountain's north slope. Along the way, it passes some forested wetlands and almost reaches the edge of Grassy Pond, which you'll be able to spot through the trees. You'll also travel over a series of bog bridges and two footbridges that span brooks. Moving away from Grassy Pond, the trail begins to climb steadily up the mountain to reach the Summit Spur Trail in 1.3 miles. The Summit Spur Trail climbs for 0.3 mile to the mountain's summit, which is marked with a large rock pile and offers a nice view of 1,300-foot-tall Ragged Mountain, topped by a radio tower.

For a shorter trek that doesn't feel quite as remote, I suggest starting at Route 17. The trail starts across the road from the parking area on Route 17, entering the forest to climb the mountain's eastern slope right away. In just 0.4 mile the trail reaches what's known as the Northern Outlook, where some people call it a day and turn around for a quick 0.8-mile out-and-back hike. This outlook offers a nice view of Ragged Mountain.

Continuing on the trail, it travels 0.2 mile along the mountain's ridge to the East Outlook, which is about 800 feet above sea level and offers an open view of Ragged Mountain, Mirror Lake, and the ocean beyond. The trail then dips down into the forest, then climbs gradually up again to reach the Summit Spur Trail in 0.3 mile. This

A pile of rocks is located at the summit at the end of the Summit Spur Trail.

section of trail between the East Outlook and West Outlook is interesting because it travels along a beautiful old rock wall that indicates the forest was once pastureland.

For more information: Visit www.georgesriver.org or call (207) 594-5166.

Personal note: March, with its dirty snow and freezing rain, certainly isn't my favorite month for hiking. But the March sun is nice—each day it climbs higher, stays out longer, and seems to burn just a little bit brighter, giving us hope that indeed, winter will end. It was that sun that drew me outdoors in late March 2014, to hike Spruce Mountain with my dog, Oreo. I chose this particular mountain because it's on the Georges Highland Path, which I'm interested in hiking in its entirety, bit by bit.

I actually drove past the trailhead for the hike on Mount Pleasant Street a few times before it caught my eye. The small wooden signs that marked the trail on both sides of the road were nearly buried in dirty snowbanks, which gave me the impression that not many people hiked the trail in the winter. But once we got going, I noticed that the trail was indeed packed down by snowshoes of other hikers. The forest was skeletal—skinny trunks and bare branches swaying in the cold wind. Sunlight reflected off the hard, thin crust of snow that covered the frozen ground.

The leaves are displaying their fall colors on Spruce Mountain in Rockport.

Oreo was especially goofy during this hike for whatever reason. He kept rolling onto his back and eating the snow. He tried to eat a cattail, then decided to go swimming in the freezing brook. Even though it seemed like the winter was dragging on that year—the high temperature that day was 33 degrees Fahrenheit—I think Oreo must have sensed that spring weather was on its way.

I didn't return to the mountain until October of 2017, and it didn't start out well. Somehow, while collecting my hiking gear, I slammed myself in the nose with my car door. I heard a crack and instantly sank to the ground, holding my poor nose, waiting for blood that didn't come. Boy, that hurt. After sniffing back a few tears, I continued packing but felt a bit shook up.

The sun heated up my black jacket as I hiked down under the power lines and into the forest. It seemed to me that much had changed since my last visit, though perhaps some of that change was simply due to the fact that there were leaves—and colorful leaves—on the trees. The trees were taller than I remembered. Could they have grown that much in three years? And the terrain seemed a bit rockier and hillier.

As I hopped between mossy boulders, I became concerned that I had hiked in the wrong direction on the Georges Highland Path, that I was instead headed

A sturdy bridge on the Georges Highland Path spans a brook at the base of Spruce Mountain.

An old rock wall is located between the east and west outlooks atop Spruce Mountain.

toward Pleasant Mountain. So about 0.4 mile into the hike, according to my GPS, I turned around, backtracked to the trailhead, and headed in the other direction. Hiking among bushes and grass, I soon realized I'd been correct the first time. Frustrated, I turned around again, heading back to the car. I could blame all this confusion on my smarting nose, but a lot of it had to do with me being overconfident about a trail I hadn't hiked in years. I should have studied the map closer and planned things more thoroughly.

Back at the car, I charged up my phone, which of course had died. There I studied the map so I could stop running around like a chicken with its head cut off. Checking my watch, I realized I only had an hour and a half before I needed to leave for an appointment that I couldn't reschedule. Now oriented on the map, I realized that (a) I'd gone the correct way the first time, and (b) I needed to hike about 3.5 miles to get to the outlooks I wanted to before my appointment. I was determined to reach those outlooks because I needed photos for this book, so I hit the trail at a jog.

Sometimes running and sometimes speed-walking, I made it to the summit of the mountain, huffing and puffing. I then sped over to the east outlook before turning around. I made it in just under one and a half hours, but it wasn't easy, and it didn't afford much time to enjoy the great views. It also didn't give me much time to engage with the chipmunk that followed me for a stretch, and it certainly didn't leave time to sit and enjoy the sound of acorns falling to the ground as the wind shook them off the trees. But I made it. I got a good workout; I photographed the views and sections of the trail I found to be especially interesting; and my nose healed up in no time.

Hike 11: Canal Path in Searsmont

Difficulty: Easy to moderate. The Canal Path is a 3-mile trail that travels over unimproved forest floor that includes plenty of rocks and tree roots, as well as narrow bog bridges that make for tricky footing in some sections. A bit north of the halfway point, the trail splits into a small loop that hikers often use as a turnaround point.

Dogs: Permitted if kept on leash

Cost: None

Access: The trail is closed to the public during deer hunting season in the fall. At all other times, the public is welcome. Overnight camping is prohibited.

Wheelchair accessibility: The trail was not constructed to be wheelchair accessible.

Hunting: Only by private landowner permission

Restrooms: None

How to get there: The north trailhead is located by Robbins Lumber. From the Fraternity Village Store in Searsmont, near the intersection of Route 131 and Route 173, head south on Route 131 for 1.7 miles to Ghent Road on the left. Travel 0.25 mile on Ghent Road to the parking area on the right, just after crossing the bridge. You will need to walk back over the bridge to reach the trailhead, which is marked with a kiosk.

The south trailhead is located at the Appleton Preserve parking area. From the intersection of Route 17 and Route 131 in Union, travel north on Route 131 for 7.8 miles. Turn right onto Route 105, and the parking area is in 0.4 mile on the right.

GPS coordinates: North trailhead, 44.335671, -69.199060; south trailhead, 44.307842, -69.215552

The Canal Path is a 3-mile hiking trail that travels through a beautiful mixed forest along the banks of the St. George River to visit what remains of the historic Georges River Canal, which dates back to the late 1700s. Along the way, interpretive displays describe aspects of the canal system that are still visible today. This trail is one of several that make up the 50-mile Georges Highland Path, a network of low-impact footpaths in the Midcoast region built and maintained by the Georges River Land Trust.

The Canal Path is located on land owned by the Robbins Lumber Company, a fifth-generation, family-owned business that started in 1881. The company owns and manages 30,000 acres and buys logs from more than 150 independent loggers. Milling operations are located on a 40-acre site in Searsmont, not far from the Canal Path.

In addition to having historic significance, the trail is also an opportunity for people to learn about local forestry practices. A trail brochure, available at the north trailhead kiosk, features a self-guided tour of the sustainable forestry practices of Robbins Lumber. Numbered signs along the trail match up with descriptions on the brochure.

Exploring the trail from the north trailhead, follow the worn footpath past the kiosk toward the forest beside the river. Just before entering the forest, you'll walk by a stone memorial bench for James F. McLarty, 1946–2007, "Friend of the River."

Marked with blue blazes, the trail weaves through tall evergreens and beds of ferns, never traveling far from the banks of the St. George River, also known as the

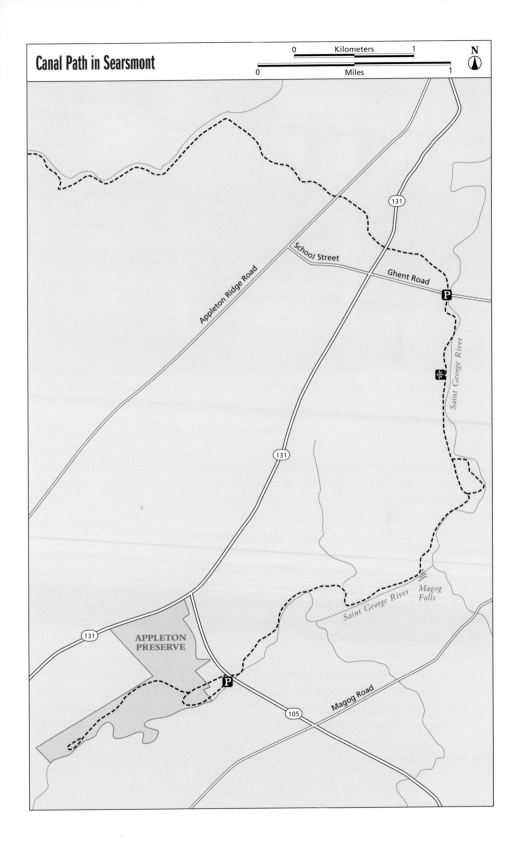

131

School Street

Appleton Ridge Road

Ghent Road

P

Saint George River

131

Saint George River   Magog Falls

131

APPLETON PRESERVE

P

105

Magog Road

A kiosk displaying a trail map and other important information about the Canal Path marks the trail's north end.

Georges River. In fact, several sections of the trail travel right along the edge of the rushing water.

The self-guided tour has seven stops, and these are all marked along the first half of the trail. About 0.6 mile from the north trailhead, you'll come to three interpretive displays about the old canal and "mystery dam." After the second display, about 0.8 mile from the north trailhead, the trail splits into a 0.6-mile loop, which can be traveled in either direction. At the far end of the loop, the trail continues along the river for another 1.6 miles to the south trailhead. Many visitors use the loop as a turnaround point, returning to the north trailhead for an out-and-back hike that is just over 2 miles long.

At both ends of the Canal Path, hikers can cross a road and continue hiking on nearby trails that are also a part of the Georges Highland Path. From the north trailhead, hikers can cross Ghent Road to explore the River to Ridge Trail; from the south trailhead, hikers can cross Route 105 to explore Appleton Preserve.

The 50-mile Georges Highland Path consists of many separate trails, the majority of which run across private land where landowners have granted the public permission to use the trails. For that reason, it's especially important that trail users stay on trail and respect the privacy of any nearby residents.

For more information: Visit www.georgesriver.org or call the Georges River Land Trust at (207) 594-5166.

Personal note: I first explored this trail with my then-boyfriend (now-husband) Derek and our dog, Oreo, in late January in 2014, on a day that had high temperatures in the mid-30s—a relatively mild day for that time of year. A thin layer of clouds covered the sky, parting on occasion to let the sun shine through.

While on the trail, we remarked on how beautiful the forest was, with multiple layers of evergreen growth and a few impressively large pines. We both decided to return in the summer, when we imagined the riverside trail would be even more enjoyable and we'd be able to get a better idea of what's left of the old canal.

Early on in the hike, we started noticing impressive holes left by resident wood-peckers, and I glimpsed the bright red crest of a pileated woodpecker as it flew over the trail.

(Skip this paragraph if you prefer not to hear about anything gory.) Beside the trail, I spied a bloody piece of white fur; the remains of a snowshoe hare is my best guess, but I'm not an expert on animal hides. My reaction to the bit of flesh and fur was more of fascination than anything else. I saw it as a small piece of evidence of the natural cycles of life and death in the forest.

Bunchberries grow in abundance along a section of the Canal Path.

The Canal Path, lined with ferns, runs along the edge of the St. George River in Searsmont.

Later in the hike, we spooked a grouse—or rather, it spooked us as it emerged out of nowhere, beating its wings frantically and flying to a safe perch. We then spooked another, and another, and another. Four grouse! Oreo strained on the leash, eager to chase the noisy birds, but we managed to keep him under control with the help of Milk-Bones.

My second Canal Path experience was a solo hike on a sunny day in July of 2017. I was in the general area to conduct an interview for my job as an outdoors reporter at the *Bangor Daily News*, and when that was wrapped up, I took a detour into Searsmont to check out the trail, which had expanded from the old canal site south to Appleton. With a camera in hand, I walked quickly along the trail, at least at first. It wasn't long before the general beauty of the forest slowed down my progress because I felt compelled to take photographs of fern-filled clearings, moss-covered stumps, and beds of bright red bunchberries.

The river that day was tranquil, its smooth surface reflecting the lush forest, and it appeared I had all of the lovely trail to myself. The only other soul I ran into was a white-tailed deer, which bounded away in the blink of an eye.

Hike 12: Cameron Mountain in Lincolnville

Difficulty: Moderate. The hike to the summit of Cameron Mountain is 5 miles out and back, and most of the hike is on smooth, wide multiuse trails that slope uphill gradually. You can lengthen the hike to about 7 miles by using the Sky Blue Trail to form a loop.

Dogs: Permitted if kept on leash

Cost: Admission varies depending on age and residency. Maine residents ages 12-64 are $4, nonresidents ages 12-64 are $6, Maine residents 65 and older are free, children ages 5-11 are $1, and children younger than 5 years old are free.

Access: The day-use areas of the park are open year-round from 9 a.m. to sunset, and visitors are required to pay a fee upon entry to the park. The parking lot is plowed in the winter.

Wheelchair accessibility: The trails were not constructed to be wheelchair accessible.

Hunting: Not permitted between June 1 and Labor Day. For the rest of the year, hunting is permitted in accordance with state laws and local ordinances. The discharge of any weapon is prohibited from or within 300 feet of any picnic area, campsite, parking area, building, posted trail, or other developed area.

Restrooms: None

How to get there: From the intersection of Route 1 and Route 173 in the town of Lincolnville, take Route 173 for 1.3 miles to an intersection. Continue straight on Route 173 (Beach Road) and drive another 0.9 mile, then turn left onto Youngtown Road. Drive just 200 feet, then turn left into the parking lot for the north entrance of Camden Hills State Park. A multiuse trail leaves this parking area.

GPS coordinates: 44.280076, -69.044700

One of the smallest peaks in the scenic Camden Hills, Cameron Mountain reaches just 811 feet above sea level. However, the top of the mountain is covered with blueberry barrens, and this low-lying vegetation allows hikers to enjoy an unobstructed 360-degree view of the region from the summit.

From the north parking lot of Camden Hills State Park in Lincolnville, the hike to the summit of Cameron Mountain starts on the wide, smooth multiuse Ski Lodge Trail, which is the only trail that leaves from the parking lot. At the trailhead is a kiosk displaying a trail map and park guidelines, and just beyond that is a sign with mileage to the many trails that spur off the Ski Lodge Trail.

Following the Ski Lodge Trail, you'll hike south, traveling gradually uphill for 1.25 miles to the Cameron Mountain Trail, which will be on your right and marked with a sign. Along the way, you'll pass the Frohock Mountain Trail on your left; this trail climbs over Derry Mountain (777 feet above sea level) and continues to the wooded summit of Frohock Mountain (454 feet above sea level) in 2.2 miles.

At 1.2 miles you'll come to the Bald Rock Mountain Trail on your left; this trail climbs steeply to the bare summit of Bald Rock Mountain. Continuing on the Ski Lodge Trail just a few steps farther, you'll come to the Cameron Mountain Trail on your right. Marked with blue blazes, the Cameron Mountain Trail is a multiuse trail, though not as wide as the Ski Lodge Trail. At its beginning, the trail dips down, then heads gradually uphill, striking west to Cameron Mountain. Highlights of this trail

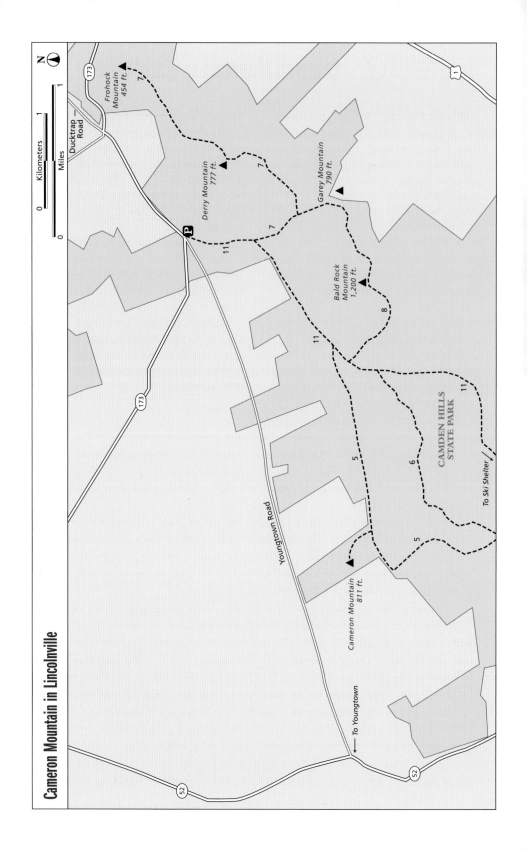

Cameron Mountain in Lincolnville

N

Kilometers
0   1

Miles
0   1

173 Frohock Mountain 454 ft. 7

Ducktrap Road

Derry Mountain 777 ft. 7

P

7

11

Garey Mountain 790 ft.

Bald Rock Mountain 1,200 ft.

8

11

11

173

5

6

CAMDEN HILLS STATE PARK

To Ski Shelter

5

5

Cameron Mountain 811 ft.

Youngtown Road

To Youngtown

52

52

1

A hiker stands near the summit of Cameron Mountain, which rises 811 feet above sea level in Camden Hills State Park.

include many beautiful old rock walls, a stand of tall white pine trees, and a small bubbling brook.

About 1 mile from the Ski Lodge Trail, the Cameron Mountain Trail comes to a side trail on the right that leads steeply through blueberry barrens to the open summit of Cameron Mountain. There is no sign marking the summit, but the top of the cone-shaped mountain is obvious. From that vantage point, hikers are rewarded with a panoramic view that includes the nearby Bald Rock, Derry, and Frohock mountains to the east; a piece of Megunticook Lake and Norton Pond to the west; and Mount Megunticook to the south.

The trail ends at the summit of Cameron Mountain. From there, hikers can retrace their steps for a 5-mile out-and-back hike, or they can continue west on the Cameron Mountain Trail, heading downhill. Soon the trail takes a sharp turn south. In about 1 mile, the trail will come to the Sky Blue Trail on the left. Take the Sky Blue Trail, which is hilly and heads northeast to meet the Ski Lodge Trail in 1.7 miles. From there, turn left on the Ski Lodge Trail and hike 1.5 miles back to the parking lot for a hike that totals about 7 miles.

For more information: Visit www.maine.gov/camdenhills or call (207) 236-3109.

Personal note: My breath lifted in a cloud as I studied the trail map on the kiosk and fastened the flaps of my fur-lined hat under my chin. The temperature was around

Ice formations adorn the edge of a brook flowing beside the Cameron Mountain Trail in December.

20 degrees Fahrenheit, but I was warm enough in layers of clothes, including thick wool socks and my favorite bright red snow pants. My husband, Derek, also wore his fur-lined bomber hat, and he carried heat packets in his backpack, just in case our fingers started to freeze.

An old sign points the way to Cameron Mountain at the north end of Camden Hills State Park.

It was a sunny day, but being so close to the winter solstice—the shortest day of the year—the sun was already ducking behind the trees at midday, casting long shadows across the wide multiuse trail. Packed snow crunched under our boots as we walked quickly uphill, our bodies gradually warming up as we neared the Cameron Mountain Trail in Camden Hills State Park.

Hearing the telltale drumming sound of a woodpecker, I paused and listened until I located the bird—a female hairy woodpecker—drilling its sharp beak into the trunk of a dead tree beside the trail. Derek helped me unearth my heavy 100-400mm camera lens from my backpack so I could snap a few photos before continuing on at a fast pace.

Bald Mountain and Frohock Mountain can be seen from atop Cameron Mountain.

As we neared the Cameron Mountain Trail, a man approached us heading in the opposite direction on a fat-tire bike, which is a mountain bike with special, wide tires that allow for better flotation on snow and other soft surfaces, such as sand. He stopped and told us a bit about Cameron Mountain. It would be windy and cold up there in the open at the summit, he warned us, but there was a nice view.

It turned out that he was right. At the rocky top of Cameron Mountain, the frigid wind took my breath away and brought tears to my eyes. We stood there for a couple minutes to take in the view, then headed back down, pausing to eat a snack beside the trail at the edge of the blueberry fields, where the wind couldn't reach us and we could enjoy the afternoon sunlight.

Hike 13: John B. Mountain in Brooksville

Difficulty: Moderate. Though this mountain is just 250 feet above sea level, the trail leading to its summit is steep for a good stretch. The interconnecting trails on the property total about 1 mile.

Dogs: Permitted if kept on leash.

Cost: None.

Access: The trails are open to foot traffic only and are open during daylight hours, year round. In the wintertime, the parking lot is plowed. Fires are not permitted.

Wheelchair accessibility: The trails were not constructed to be wheelchair accessible.

Hunting: Permitted in accordance to state laws.

Restrooms: None.

How to get there: From the intersection of Route 175 and Route 176 in Brooksville, take Route 176 (Coastal Road) and drive 3.8 miles. Turn left onto Breezemere Road and drive 0.8 mile to the trailhead and a small parking lot, which will be on your right. If the lot is full, there is a larger parking lot about 0.2 mile north on Breezemere Road (back the way you came). These parking lots may not be plowed in the winter.

GPS coordinates: 44.344922, -68.760015

John B. Mountain is a small mountain, rising just 250 feet above sea level in Brooksville. Yet from its partially open summit and rocky ledges, hikers are rewarded with stunning views of Eggemoggin Reach, Blue Hill Mountain, and the Camden Hills. This mountain was donated to the Blue Hill Heritage Trust by Joel and Rush Davis in 2009 in a 38-acre parcel, which now is home to a simple network of blazed hiking trails that total just over 1 mile. These trails not only explore the forested slopes and rocky top of John B. Mountain, they also visit the nearby Long Cove of Eggemoggin Reach.

At the trailhead is a kiosk that displays a laminated trail map and information about the trails, as well as a cubby that contains a register for visitors to sign.

The trails in the network form a big loop called the Outer Loop, which is 0.75 mile long. Along that loop, the trail splits near the top of the mountain, then comes back together near the summit. At the summit, there is a small loop that leads hikers to a few different outlooks.

The newest addition to the trail network is the 0.2 mile Long Cove Path, added in 2017. This trail branches off the Outer Loop at the base of the mountain and runs south, traveling over a trail easement area to end at Long Cove of Eggemoggin Reach.

One potentially confusing aspect of the hike is that the different trails that make up the Outer Loop have a few different names. Starting at the trailhead kiosk, the wide trail to the left is known as School House Road. You would start on that trail to hike the Outer Loop clockwise. School House Road travels along the bottom of the steep west slope of John B. Mountain through a mixed forest. About 0.15 mile from the trailhead, Long Cove Path veers off to your left. Continuing on School House Road, at about 0.3 mile from the trailhead, it comes to an intersection. If you

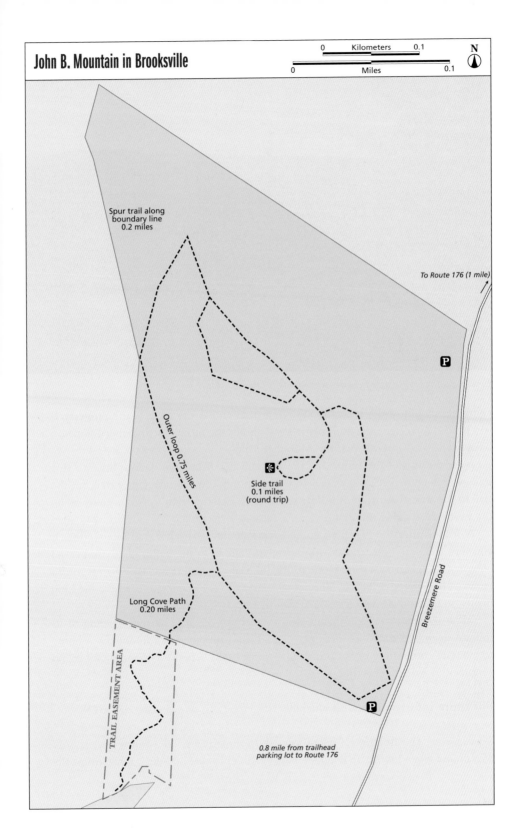

John B. Mountain in Brooksville

0 Kilometers 0.1

0 Miles 0.1

N

To Route 176 (1 mile)

Spur trail along
boundary line
0.2 miles

Outer loop 0.75 miles

Side trail
0.1 miles
(round trip)

Long Cove Path
0.20 miles

TRAIL EASEMENT AREA

Breezemere Road

0.8 mile from trailhead
parking lot to Route 176

P

P

Eggemoggin Reach is seen from an overlook atop John B. Mountain.

continue straight, you'll walk 0.2 mile to a dead end at the edge of the property. If you instead turn right, the trail narrows and climbs the mountain's northern slope on what is known as the Around the Mountain Trail.

Near the top of the mountain, the Around the Mountain Trail splits into two trails, which come back together before the summit. You can take either trail, but the trail to the west (your right if hiking the loop clockwise) leads to better views along the west ledges of the mountain.

Not long after the two trails come back together is another trail intersection. If you turn left, you'll descend the mountain and return to the trailhead. If you instead continue straight, you'll soon come to the 0.1 mile Summit Loop that brings you to views of Eggemoggin Reach. The actual summit of the mountain is where the loop begins and is marked with a wooden sign that reads "Summit."

Although it's a small mountain, don't underestimate it. The trails leading to its top are steep and rocky in some places, and the summit of the mountain is home to a fragile community of various shrubs, mosses, and lichens. The mountain is also abundant in wild blueberries.

For more information: Visit bluehillheritagetrust.org or call (207) 374-5118.

Personal note: The first time I hiked John B. Mountain was on a sunny day in early March, and when I woke up that morning, I hadn't planned on hiking. I had originally intended to go cross-country skiing, but my plans abruptly changed when I sat down on the couch to drink my tea.

As I sat there in the morning sunlight, my dog, Oreo, jumped up on the couch and thoroughly smothered me with his warm little body. It didn't take long for me to cave in and start to make new plans, ones that could include Oreo. I simply couldn't leave him behind. So instead of a ski trip, I chose to snowshoe up the dog-friendly John B. Mountain.

The two parking lots for the trail network weren't plowed, so I parked on the side of the road, leaving room for traffic, and clambered over a monstrous snowbank to reach the trailhead. Oreo followed in my snowshoe tracks. According to the trail register, Oreo and I were the first visitors to the mountain since December, so we had some work ahead of us. Packing down several months' worth of snow, we made our way down the School House Road.

The snow stuck to my snowshoes as the temperature climbed to nearly 40 degrees Fahrenheit. Oreo and I both shed our coats before turning onto Around the Mountain Trail and starting the steep upward climb through a dark, dense forest where snow melting off branches rained down on our heads.

A dark-eyed junco perches in a white pine tree on John B. Mountain.

A cairn marks a trail atop John B. Mountain.

Atop the ledges on the west side of the mountain, I packed down a spot for us to sit and enjoy the view. We then continued on to the Summit Loop Trail, which leads to the best views of the hike, before retracing our steps down the mountain.

We chose that particular route because someone (perhaps a trail maintainer) left a message on the trail register warning hikers that blowdowns were blocking the narrower trail, which passes the old cemetery. I wasn't too disappointed about that — I'm sure the snow was hiding the tombstones anyway.

After visiting the small mountain, I can see why the Davises would choose to donate the land to BHHT, thus preserving it for future generations to enjoy. When standing on the summit and taking in the views, I felt that the mountain was much taller than 250 feet above sea level. I would suggest this short hike to anyone who doesn't mind a few steep slopes. I returned to the mountain years later, in the middle of the summer, and hiked it with Oreo and my husband, Derek. It was interesting to see all that had been hidden by the snow, including giant beds of moss and lichen on the forested slopes of the mountain, and a sea of low-bush blueberry bushes covering the top of the mountain.

Hike 14: Peter's Brook Trail in Blue Hill

Difficulty: Easy to moderate. The hike is 1 mile out and back. The trail travels gradually uphill as it moves away from the trailhead. Exposed tree roots, rocky areas, and a few muddy areas make footing tricky in some spots.

Dogs: Permitted if kept on leash

Cost: None

Access: The trail is open during daylight hours year-round. It is for foot traffic only. Fires, camping, and bikes are prohibited.

Wheelchair accessibility: The trail was not constructed to be wheelchair accessible.

Hunting: Only with private landowner permission

Restrooms: None

How to get there: From the intersection of Route 172 and Route 176 (also known as East Blue Hill Road) in Blue Hill, drive east on Route 176 for 0.6 mile, then park on your right at the AB Herrick Memorial Landing on Peters Cove. The trailhead is across the road from the parking area, on the east side of the bridge over Peters Brook (from the parking area, you'll need to cross the bridge). It is marked with a blue and white Blue Hill Heritage Trust sign.

GPS coordinates: 44.414358, -68.571738

Traveling through a mossy evergreen forest, the 0.5-mile Peter's Brook Trail follows the lively Peters Brook uphill from the ocean to a beautiful waterfall. Constructed and maintained by the Blue Hill Heritage Trust, the trail crosses privately owned land that is protected by conservation easements, as well as property owned by the land trust.

Your adventure will begin at the parking lot at the AB Herrick Memorial Landing, a piece of property on Peters Cove that is owned by the Blue Hill Heritage Trust and is open to the public for picnicking and launching kayaks and other small boats. The landing is a combination of sandy beach and rocky shoreline.

Across the road and across the bridge, the Peter's Brook Trail begins by descending gently into a mature forest. Just a short distance from the trailhead, you'll come to a kiosk that includes a trail map and visitor registration book.

Following Peters Brook, the trail travels through a forest composed mostly of conifers—spruce, white pine, hemlock, balsam fir, and cedar trees—with a few oak trees scattered throughout. Growing under the shade of these trees, an abundance of mosses and hardy low-lying plants carpet the forest floor.

Draining from the uplands east of Blue Hill village, Peters Brook (sometimes called Big Peters Brook) tumbles through the forest to empty into Peters Cove, which is a part of Blue Hill Bay. Little Peters Brook also empties into the cove. Along the hike, a few informal side trails here and there will bring you down to the edge of the water, where you can view several tiny waterfalls and churning pools.

The trail ends at an unnamed waterfall, where whitewater tumbles down over a steep set of natural rock steps to plunge into a calm shallow pool below.

Peter's Brook Trail in Blue Hill

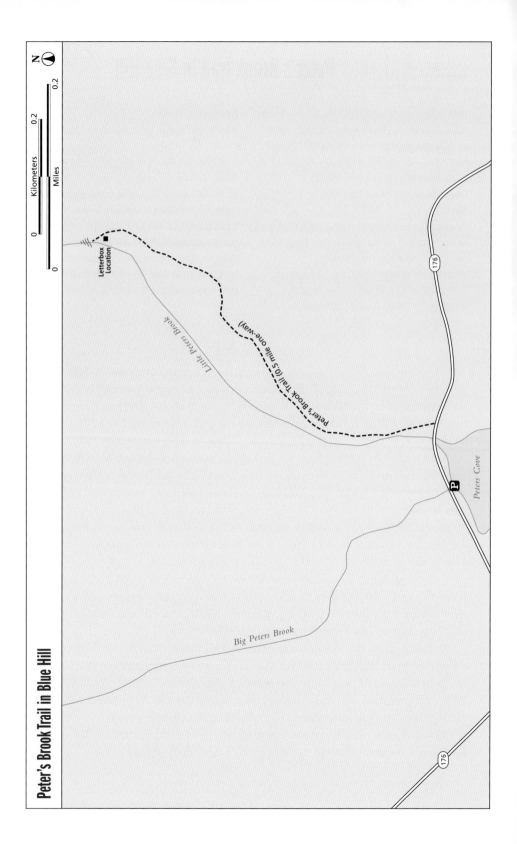

A waterfall on Peters Brook marks the far end of the Peter's Brook Trail in Blue Hill.

In my search for background information about the property, I learned Blue Hill was founded in the mid-1700s, and John Peters was among the town's earliest settlers, according to the Blue Hill Historical Society. A noted land surveyor, Peters moved to Blue Hill in 1765, and by 1790 his estate was the largest in town, consisting of 35 acres of copper mining land, 35 acres of pasture, and 1,692 acres of wildland. Throughout his years in Blue Hill, Peters became a builder and owner of ships, and he was involved in a local sawmill and gristmill. In 1815 he built a mansion atop a hill on Peters Point, west of Peters Cove. That building is now listed on the National Register of Historic Places.

For more information: Visit bluehillheritagetrust.org or call (207) 374-5118.

Personal note: It certainly didn't seem like mid-December when my husband, Derek, and I walked the Peter's Brook Trail with our dog, Oreo. The sun was shining and the temperature hovered in the 40s, rendering our winter hats and mittens unnecessary. Oreo, looking handsome in his new blaze-orange Buff bandana, didn't even need to wear a coat—aside from his permanent coat of short white and black fur, that is.

Honestly, I chose the Peter's Brook Trail because it was short and near our home. We had a family Christmas shopping trip planned for that afternoon, so we didn't have much time for outdoor adventuring. Lucky for us, the trail turned out to be much more beautiful than I expected. The evergreen forest was truly "ever green," even during that bleak time of year, when most of the world in Maine is composed of

Moss lines much of the trail.

grays and browns. Crows raised a racket from the treetops, and red squirrels wandered up to us, chattering loudly and waving their bushy tails.

The nameless waterfall at the end of the trail was much grander than I expected. At its base, I carefully balanced on slick, algae-covered rocks, risking a cold plunge into the shallows to photograph the water at different angles. Fortunately, I didn't slip. Though the weather had been unseasonably warm for December, it wasn't quite swimming weather . . . though Oreo would beg to differ. He had a nice dip before we walked back to trailhead.

Trail signs posted by the Blue Hill Heritage Trust direct hikers along the 0.5-mile Peter's Brook Trail.

Hike 15: Mead Mountain in Orland

Difficulty: Easy to moderate. If you park at the Mead Mountain Trailhead, the hike is 2.8 miles out and back; if you park at the South Gate of the Hothole Valley Parcel, the hike is 5.4 miles out and back. The roads and trails leading to the mountain and on the mountain are gradual and fairly smooth.

Dogs: Permitted if kept on leash

Cost: None

Access: Valley Road and the multiuse section of the Mead Mountain Trail are open to hikers, mountain bikers, cross-country skiers, and horseback riders. They are closed to ATVs and snowmobiles, though snowmobiles are permitted on another section of Valley Road. The last 0.6 mile of the Mead Mountain Trail is for foot traffic only.

Wheelchair accessibility: The trails were not constructed to be wheelchair accessible.

Hunting: Permitted through a registration process with the Great Pond Mountain Land Trust

Restrooms: None on the route of this hike; however, there is an outhouse on Valley Road about a mile north of the road's intersection with the Mead Mountain Trail.

How to get there: From the intersection of Route 15 and Route 1 (Acadia Highway) in Orland, drive east on Route 1 for 4.1 miles; the South Gate of Great Pond Mountain Wildlands' Hothole Valley Parcel is on your left.

This gate is open to traffic on weekends only, mid-June through Oct. If you plan your hike when the gate is open, you can drive into the Wildlands on the gravel Valley Road to the Mead Mountain Trail, which is 1.3 miles past the gate and will be on your left.

If you plan your hike when the South Gate is closed, you will simply have to park in the gravel parking area outside the gate and walk to the Mead Mountain Trailhead on Valley Road. Along the way, you'll pass Popple Grove and the trailheads of Esker Path, Drumlin Path, Oak Hill, and Hillside Trail.

GPS coordinates: South Gate, 44.568123, -68.631802; Mead Mountain Trailhead, 44.584738, -68.641521

Mead Mountain is a small mountain, rising just 660 feet above sea level in East Orland. But from dramatic ledges near its summit, hikers are rewarded with open views of Hothole Valley and the small mountains and hills beyond.

The mountain can be hiked on roads and trails located in the Great Pond Mountain Wildlands, 4,500 acres of conserved land in Orland that is owned and maintained by the Great Pond Mountain Conservation Trust. Known to locals as "the Wildlands," this property is split into two parcels: the 3,420-acre Hothole Valley Parcel and the 1,075-acre Dead River Section. Mead Mountain is located in the Hothole Valley Parcel.

To hike Mead Mountain, you should start at the South Gate of the Hothole Valley Parcel. From there, you will either walk, bike, or drive your vehicle (if the gate is open) into the Wildlands on the gravel Valley Road. Keep in mind that this road is open to all sorts of recreationists, including horseback riders and mountain bikers, and in the winter, skiers and snowmobilers. No ATVs, dirt bikes, or other off-road vehicles are allowed.

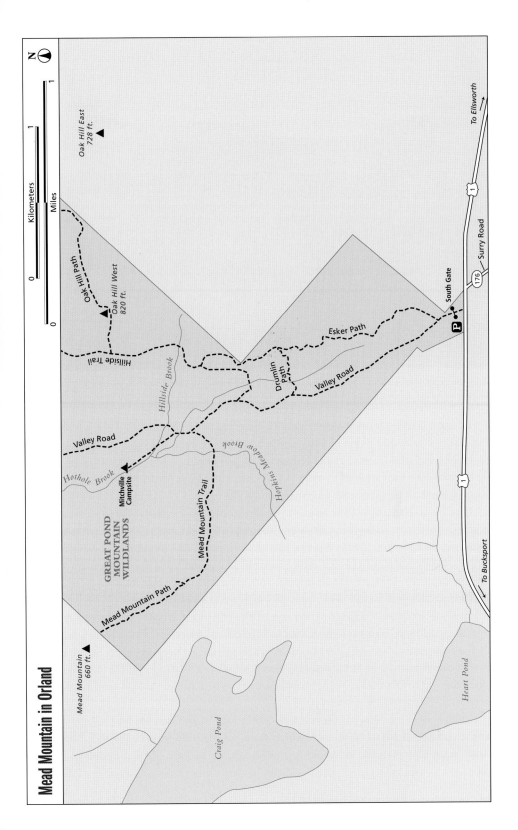

Mead Mountain in Orland

Fall foliage is at its peak in mid-October, enhancing the beauty of the view from the ledges near the top of Mead Mountain.

About 1.3 miles from the gate, turn left onto the Mead Mountain Trail, which is closed to all vehicular traffic and is actually an old road. The trail starts by climbing a fairly steep hill, then evens off and crosses a wooden bridge near a small wetland area. At 0.8 mile the trail appears to split. To the left is the new Mead Mountain Path, a narrow footpath marked with blue diamond blazes.

The Mead Mountain Path officially opened to the public in the fall of 2016 and is approximately 0.6 mile long. Traveling through a mixed forest of mostly hardwood trees, the trail leads gradually up the southeast slope of the mountain, passing two large boulders before reaching a cairn (rock pile) in a small clearing. From there, the trail descends to a viewpoint atop ledges on the east side of the mountain, where you'll find a log and sizable rock, both of which make suitable seats.

In October 2016 a trail along the top of the cliffs to the right was flagged with pink flagging tape. This route may turn into an official trail (that would form a loop) in the near future, according to Wildlands steward Brian Keegstra. The board and staff of the Wildlands are still discussing that possibility. The danger of hikers walking along the top of the cliffs is a chief concern. So if you do decide to explore this unofficial trail, exercise extreme caution.

Unlike most mountain trails, the Mead Mountain Path does not lead all the way to the summit of Mead Mountain, which is on private property according to Wildlands maps. However, the viewpoint on the ledges make for a good endpoint to the hike.

Great Pond Mountain Wildlands is the largest property conserved by the Great Pond Mountain Conservation Trust, a nonprofit organization founded in 1993 to conserve the land, water, and wildlife habitat for the communities of northwestern Hancock County. The organization also owns two small properties in Bucksport and holds conservation easements on properties in Orland and Dedham.

For more information: Visit www.greatpondtrust.org, email info@greatpondtrust.org, or call (207) 469-6929.

Personal note: "Oooo, there's the view. This is nice, huh, Orie?" I said to my dog as we reached the top of the ledges on Mead Mountain. (If you spend enough time in the woods with your pet, you end up speaking to said pet in full sentences. It's only natural—and slightly embarrassing when someone catches you doing it.)

Both Oreo and I wore bright fleece jackets that day, which was decidedly fall. A cool wind kept the temperature in the low 50s, though the sun offered some warmth. Throughout the hike, we spied a number of birds that appeared to be eating gravel on

Blue signs and flagging tape mark the hiking trail up Mead Mountain in the Great Pond Mountain Wildlands.

The multiuse Valley Road leads to many hiking trails in the Great Pond Mountain Wildlands, including the hiking trail that climbs Mead Mountain.

Valley Road; they flew up into the trees along the road as we approached, but I was able to identify blue jays, dark-eyed juncos, and a yellow-rumped warbler.

As is often the case in the fall, the brilliant foliage was a highlight of the hike. I paused several times to inspect the dying leaves—giant orange oak leaves, yellow gray birch leaves with their jagged edges, and yellow maple leaves covered with brilliant red blotches. We only have a few weeks to enjoy them, then it's time to get the rake out.

Though we walked from the South Gate, making for a 5.4-mile hike, it didn't seem that long because much of the hike was along a fairly flat, smooth road. The new trail was well built and marked, making it easy to follow, and the views at the end were much nicer than I expected, it being at such a low elevation. From the top of the ledges, I could see nothing but hills of orange, yellow, red, and the dark green of pine, spruce, and fir that never leaves Maine's landscape, no matter the time of year.

Hike 16: Green Lake Nature Trails in Ellsworth

Difficulty: Easy to moderate. The trail network consists of the 1.35-mile Hastings Trail, as well as a side trail to the hatchery. Both trails travel through a mixed forest over fairly even terrain. Exposed tree roots, wooden bridges, and a few rocky areas may make footing tricky from time to time.

Dogs: Permitted if kept on leash

Cost: None

Access: The trails are for foot traffic only and are open year-round during daylight hours. The parking area outside the hatchery gate is plowed during the winter.

Wheelchair accessibility: The trails were not constructed to be wheelchair accessible.

Hunting: Not permitted

Restrooms: None

How to get there: From the intersection of Route 180 and Route 1A in Ellsworth (the entrance of Boggy Brook Business Park), drive 4.2 miles on Route 180 (also known as Mariaville Road), then turn left onto Hatchery Way, the entrance for the Green Lake National Fish Hatchery. At the beginning of Hatchery Way, park outside the gate, to the side, well out of the way of traffic. The gate is closed and locked at 4 p.m. most days, but sometimes earlier.

GPS coordinates: 44.624170, -68.435400

Ghost towns, glaciers, and freshwater ecosystems are three topics you'll learn about while walking the Green Lake Nature Trails in Ellsworth. Just under 2 miles in total length, these walking trails travel through the quiet forest surrounding the Green Lake National Fish Hatchery and visit the shore of Green Lake. Along the way, a few informational displays help visitors interpret the landscape.

The trail network, completed in the fall of 2015, consists of two trails: the main trail, called the Hastings Trail, and a side trail that leads to the hatchery. The trails are marked with small green diamond-shaped signs posted to trees.

Starting outside the hatchery gate at a trailhead kiosk, the Hastings Trail travels through the woods south of the hatchery for about 1.35 miles to reach the southeast shore of Green Lake, where it ends at a beautiful granite memorial bench for Ed Hastings, whom the trail is named for. An environmental scientist, Hastings was an officer of the nonprofit Friends of Green Lake National Fish Hatchery and worked with salmon on the Penobscot River as a contractor for NOAA Fisheries in Orono. He passed away in 2006.

From the bench, visitors can watch for bald eagles, which are often seen perched in nearby white pine trees, fishing the waters of Green Lake.

Informational displays are spaced out along the Hastings Trail. Starting at the trailhead, the first display is about glacial erratics, boulders left on the landscape by receding glaciers during the last ice age. The trail travels past many of these interesting rocks.

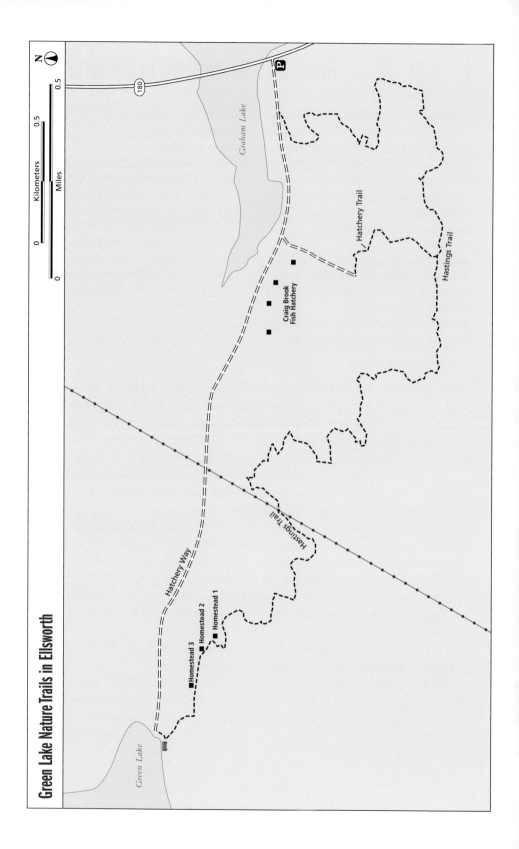

Green Lake Nature Trails in Ellsworth

Green Lake

Homestead 3
Homestead 2
Homestead 1

Hatchery Way

Hastings Trail

Hastings Trail

Craig Brook
Fish Hatchery

Hatchery Trail

Hastings Trail

Graham Lake

180

P

N

Kilometers
0   0.5
Miles
0   0.5

A short distance past the glacial erratics display, a side trail to the hatchery splits off to your right. This trail leads to the hatchery buildings and the hatchery road, which you can follow back to the trailhead for a 0.77-mile loop hike.

However, if you continue following the Hastings Trail, you'll soon pass vernal pools, temporary pools of water that are important habitats for certain animals, such as salamanders, fairy shrimp, and frogs. These special pools will be located to your left, but may be dried up, depending on the time of year.

After crossing a few wooden bridges and winding around several boulders, the trail crosses a power-line corridor, where you'll find low-lying bushes, mosses, and lichens. Since this corridor is cleared of trees, this section of trail is marked by little rock piles called cairns. At this point you are more than halfway to the lake.

Beyond the power lines, the trail travels through a shady stand of evergreens and past the remains of three homesteads. Only the cellar holes and a few rusted relics remain of what were once family homes near the shore of Green Lake. By the third cellar hole is an informational sign about this little "ghost town."

The last informational display is located at the memorial bench near the lakeshore and is about Maine's freshwater ecosystems.

The Hastings Trail at the Green Lake National Fish Hatchery ends at the southeast shore of Green Lake, where a dam is located.

An educational display on the Hastings Trail at the Green Lake National Fish Hatchery describes a "ghost town," the remains of several old homesteads located near the trail.

Just before the bench, a spur trail leads visitors over a wooden walkway to a dam and the end of the hatchery road. Visitors are welcome to walk along the paved road (rather than backtrack on the trail) to make their hike a 1.83-mile loop.

Construction of the Green Lake Nature Trails was a joint effort by multiple organizations and government bodies, which are posted at the trailhead. Pete Coleman from Pathmaker Trail Services was instrumental in the trails' design and construction, as were many volunteers.

The Green Lake National Fish Hatchery is involved in restoring Atlantic salmon, which is one the nation's most significantly depleted fish species, according to the US Fish and Wildlife Service. Work at the hatchery includes producing smolts (young salmon) for distribution into select rivers in Maine and New Hampshire. The hatchery also conducts field research to assess populations.

For more information: Call the Green Lake National Fish Hatchery at (207) 667-9531.

Personal note: In mid-October, the Hastings Trail was covered with what looked like bright yellow polka dots—the round, serrated leaves of bigtooth aspen, occasionally mixed with the large pale yellow leaves of striped maple. I walked the trail slowly, enjoying the colors—rusty orange and green splotched with rich red, like drops of

◀ *Colorful leaves litter the Green Lake Nature Trails in October.*

blood. The forest floor changed under my feet, first a carpet of golden red oak leaves; next a carpet of long, orange pine needles dotted with bright red maple leaves; and after that, a carpet of crispy beech leaves fringed by shrunken ferns, painted in gold.

I was intrigued by the variety, but my dog, Oreo, was less interested. He wanted to go, go, go.

It was 2015, and the trail was about 95 percent complete. Having spied the trailhead kiosk beside the road, I'd jumped the gun and decided to explore it before the network's grand opening. The trails had already been well-packed by work crews and local residents, and flagging tape and trail signs marked the way.

During the hike, we ran into a man who was working on the trail, constructing beautiful wooden bridges and walkways, installing stone steps, and smoothing out especially uneven sections of the trail. Over Oreo's rude barking, he let me know about a hollow maple up ahead, in which mushrooms grew. Noticing the camera hanging from my neck, he figured I'd want to take a photo, and he was right. When we found the tree, Oreo tried to crawl inside while I snapped several photos of the whimsical site—dozens of tiny capped mushrooms sprouting from the dead wood.

At the end of the hike, on the shore of Green Lake, I spotted an immature bald eagle sitting high up in a pine tree by the water. I knew it was a young eagle because its feathers were a mix of dark brown, medium brown, and white. It takes bald eagles about five years to develop their adult plumage—a solid brown body with a white tail and white head. Until that time, they tend to fly under the radar and many people mistake them for hawks.

A juvenile bald eagle perches in a white pine tree at the Green Lake National Fish Hatchery.

Hike 17: Mariaville Falls Preserve in Mariaville

Difficulty: Moderate. The trails on the preserve total about 1.4 miles and travel over hills and along a steep slope. For an unobstructed view of the falls, you must take a side trail that is extremely steep and rocky.

Dogs: Permitted but must be kept under voice control at all times

Cost: None

Access: Authorized uses for the preserve are canoeing, kayaking, fishing, hiking, and nature observation. The trails are for foot traffic only. The road and parking lot may or may not be plowed. Call the Frenchman Bay Conservancy to check the road's status in the winter.

Wheelchair accessibility: The trails were not constructed to be wheelchair accessible.

Hunting: Permitted in accordance with state laws

Restrooms: None

How to get there: From Route 1 in north Ellsworth, turn right onto Mariaville Road. In just a few feet, you'll pass Boggy Brook Road, the entrance to Ellsworth Business Park, on your left. Drive 8.3 miles on Mariaville Road, then turn right onto Route 181 (just past the Beech Hill School). Drive on Route 181 for 9.7 miles and turn left onto a gravel access road to Mariaville Falls Preserve. The access road is marked by a large wooden sign for the preserve. Drive about 0.2 mile to the first parking lot and the trailhead to what's known as the New Trail, which travels through the forest 0.48 mile to connect to the Fisherman's Trail south of Mariaville Falls; or continue up the road about 0.1 mile to the second parking lot at a gravel pit and the trailhead to the Fisherman's Trail, which traces the river to Mariaville Falls.

GPS coordinates: First trailhead, 44.797126, -68.386235; second trailhead, 44.797347, -68.387678

Mariaville Falls Preserve, which officially opened to the public in October of 2015, features 1.4 miles of hiking trails that lead to scenic stair falls on the West Branch of the Union River. The Frenchman Bay Conservancy pieced together the preserve with two land purchases that total 123 acres on the east shore of the river, and one conservation easement on 18 acres across the river, on the west shore. The conservancy then designed two trails on the property.

The 0.85-mile Fisherman's Trail starts at a gravel pit and descends a slope to the West Branch of the Union River. The trail then turns right to travel upriver to Mariaville Falls. Along the way, the trail travels up and over several hills and traces the top of a steep slope to visit viewpoints along the scenic river.

The trail soon approaches Mariaville Falls, which is really a series of waterfalls known as a "staircase falls." This section of whitewater can be viewed from an overlook on the trail, or hikers can get a closer look by descending a rough, steep side trail to the rocks at the bottom of the falls.

The Fisherman's Trail continues past the falls to a bend in the river, where there's a nice flat spot near the edge of the water for picnicking. At this spot, a sign is posted on a tree warning paddlers of the waterfall downriver.

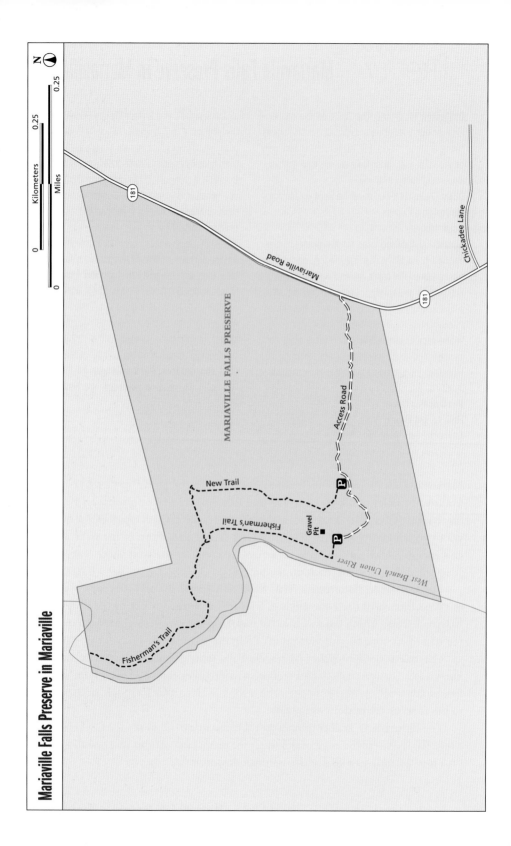

Mariaville Falls Preserve in Mariaville

Mariaville Falls, a dramatic stair falls on the West Branch of the Union River, shines in the late September sun in Mariaville Falls Preserve.

The second trail on the property is yet to be named and is 0.48 mile long. On trail maps, it's labeled as "New Trail." Starting at the first parking area of the preserve, the trail travels through the woods and descends a hill to connect with the Fisherman's Trail south of Mariaville Falls. To reach the falls, turn right onto the Fisherman's Trail and hike a couple tenths of a mile.

While following the trails through the shaded evergreen forest, it's hard to imagine that the land was once the location of a village. In the early 1800s, William Bingham of Philadelphia established a settlement at Mariaville Falls, and it grew to include a dam, two timber mills, a tannery, a boardinghouse, and homes for about 50 families, according to the Frenchman Bay Conservancy. Today there are no noticeable traces of this village along the preserve trails.

The Frenchman Bay Conservancy is a nationally accredited, nonprofit land conservation organization, founded in 1987 by a group of local residents concerned about the development threat to Donnell Pond in Sullivan. The organization broadened its scope over the years, and to date has protected nearly 7,000 acres in 12 towns and townships through conservation easements or by purchasing the properties and establishing preserves. On these properties, the organization maintains more than 25 miles of hiking trails, including the trails leading to Mariaville Falls.

For more information: Visit www.frenchmanbay.org or call (207) 422-2328.

A toad pauses while hopping along the forest floor of Mariaville Falls Preserve in late September.

Personal note: Joined by my husband, Derek, and our dog, Oreo, I visited Mariaville Falls Preserve on September 27, 2015, just before its grand opening in early October. It turned out to be great weather for hiking. It was a crisp fall day, but the sun was warm enough for us to shed our fleece jackets while snacking on the rocks near the falls.

Mushrooms grow on a tree in Mariaville Falls Preserve.

The trails were marked with blue flagging tape tied around tree trunks, but the conservancy staff told me the tape would soon be replaced with either blue-painted blazes or tiny square signs nailed to trees. I've seen both methods used to mark trails of other Frenchman Bay Conservancy lands.

We were the only visitors to the preserve that afternoon. Chickadees sang to us as we walked through the shady forest. We paused to photograph an American toad, white tree mushrooms, and shiny brown-capped mushrooms growing up out of the forest floor.

The river frothed and roared at the stair falls, which I imagine looks very different when the water is higher in the spring. Both above and below the falls, the river appeared quite different. Lined with tall grasses, the river's clear water

A hiker follows the Fisherman's Trail. The land slopes down to the West Branch of the Union River.

flowed slowly. Its surface was smooth, disturbed only by darting water beetles. Enjoying the peacefulness of the spot, we lingered at the preserve for several hours. We knew it would be one of the last days of the year warm enough for us to wear T-shirts and watch Oreo splash in the water.

Hike 18: Jordan Cliffs Trail in Acadia National Park on Mount Desert Island

Difficulty: Moderate to strenuous, depending on whether you're afraid of heights. Round-trip from Jordan Pond House, loop hikes with the ascent being on the 1.4-mile Jordan Cliffs Trail vary from 3.7 miles to 5.7 miles, depending on whether you want to bag one peak (Penobscot Mountain) or two peaks (Penobscot and Sargent Mountains). This trail includes iron rungs, narrow bridges, rocky sections, granite staircases, tangles of exposed tree roots, and short, steep areas that require hand-over-foot climbing.

Dogs: Not permitted. While leashed dogs are allowed on most trails in Acadia National Park, this trail is off-limits to dogs because it includes iron rungs (which dogs cannot climb) and cliffs (which can be dangerous for dogs).

Cost: All visitors to Acadia are required to pay an entrance fee May through Oct. These fees vary in cost, with most visitors purchasing a vehicle pass for $25, which is good for 7 days. However, if you visit the park often, you may as well purchase an annual pass for $50. Park passes are available at several locations in and near the park, including park visitor centers. They can also be purchased online at www.nps .gov/acad.

Access: The trail is for foot traffic only, though the carriage roads you walk on for a short distance on your way to the trail are open to bicycling and horseback riding. The Jordan Cliffs Trail is often closed mid-March through early August to protect the peregrine falcons nesting on the cliffs. In the winter, the Jordan Pond area is accessible by Jordan Pond Road; all other access points aren't plowed. However, the Jordan Cliffs Trail would be very dangerous to hike when covered in ice and snow.

Wheelchair accessibility: The trails were not constructed to be wheelchair accessible.

Hunting: Not permitted

Restrooms: A vault toilet is located at the Jordan Pond boat launch area and is open year-round. In addition, there are bathrooms at the Jordan Pond Restaurant, which are generally only open when the restaurant is open.

How to get there: The closest parking area to the Jordan Cliffs Trail is at Jordan Pond off the Park Loop Road. This parking lot fills up quickly, especially during the weekend in the summer and fall. To avoid being turned away due to lack of parking, arrive early in the morning, plan the hike on a weekday or during the off-season (spring and late fall), or hop on an Island Explorer bus.

To get there, drive onto Mount Desert Island on Route 3 and veer left at the intersection to drive toward Bar Harbor. After driving 7.6 miles, turn right to enter Acadia National Park at the Hulls Cove Visitor Center. Drive straight ahead for a few hundred feet; then at the intersection, turn left onto the Park Loop Road (the Hulls Cove Visitor Center and a large parking area will be to the right if you need to pay for a park pass or purchase a trail map). Drive on the Park Loop Road for 3 miles, then veer right and continue on the Park Loop Road for another 4.4 miles to the parking area for Jordan Pond on the right.

Using a detailed park trail map, navigate the carriage roads south about 0.2 mile to the Spring Trail, then hike 0.3 west to a carriage road, where you turn right to find the Jordan Cliffs Trailhead.

GPS coordinates: 44.321886, -68.260083

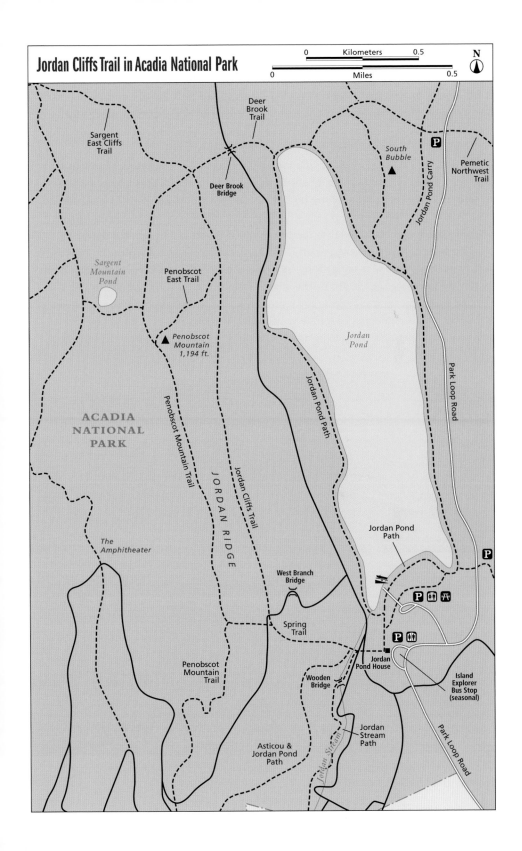

Jordan Cliffs Trail in Acadia National Park

Kilometers
0   0.5

Miles
0   0.5

N

Sargent East Cliffs Trail

Deer Brook Trail

Deer Brook Bridge

South Bubble

Jordan Pond Carry

Pemetic Northwest Trail

Sargent Mountain Pond

Penobscot East Trail

Penobscot Mountain 1,194 ft.

ACADIA NATIONAL PARK

Penobscot Mountain Trail

Jordan Cliffs Trail

J O R D A N   R I D G E

Jordan Pond Path

Jordan Pond

Park Loop Road

The Amphitheater

Jordan Pond Path

West Branch Bridge

Spring Trail

Penobscot Mountain Trail

Wooden Bridge

Jordan Pond House

Island Explorer Bus Stop (seasonal)

Jordan Stream Path

Asticou & Jordan Pond Path

Jordan Stream

Park Loop Road

The Jordan Cliffs Trail, climbing diagonally up the steep eastern side of Penobscot Mountain, is one of the most challenging and exciting trails in Acadia National Park. It offers stunning views of Jordan Pond and beyond, to Seal Harbor and the Cranberry Islands. However, because this trail is tucked away on the park's carriage roads, it's often overlooked by park visitors. It also tends to be overshadowed by two other cliff trails in the park: the Precipice Trail and the Beehive Trail.

Measuring 1.4 miles in length, the Jordan Cliffs Trail is ever-changing, presenting different challenges, including a section of metal rungs and rails that hikers must use to scale the steepest section of the trail. The trail is not for those who are afraid of heights, since a good portion travels along the edge of the cliff, with a sheer drop on one side and a rock wall rising on the other side. It is also not a place for dogs.

The nearest parking to the Jordan Cliffs Trail is at Jordan Pond House. It's important to keep in mind that the parking lots around Jordan Pond House fill up quickly in the summertime, especially in the middle of the day and on weekends. That's because this is the closest parking for several other trails, including the scenic Jordan Pond Trail, trails exploring two mountains called the Bubbles, a trail leading up the south ridge of Pemetic Mountain, and the Penobscot Mountain Trail. And being a

The author hikes up a steep section of the Jordan Cliffs Trail on Penobscot Mountain in Acadia National Park. Below is Jordan Pond.

Derek hikes along the Jordan Cliffs Trail, following the blue blazes that mark the trail.

restaurant, Jordan Pond House also attracts customers, many of which are there to enjoy the establishment's famous popovers.

To reach the Jordan Cliffs Trail from Jordan Pond House, use a map to find the nearby network of carriage roads and follow them south about 0.2 mile to the Spring Trail. On the Spring Trail, hike 0.3 mile west to another carriage road, where you'll turn right to find the Jordan Cliffs Trailhead, which is marked with a wooden sign.

The Jordan Cliffs Trail starts out by gradually climbing through a forest of spruce, cedar, and pine. But early on is a warning of the more challenging hiking ahead: a wooden sign that warns hikers that the trail is steep with exposed cliffs and fixed iron rungs.

As the trail climbs Penobscot Mountain's east side, it travels over exposed granite spotted with colorful lichen. Ducking in and out of the shaded forest, it isn't long before cliffs rise up to your left. In the summer, take a close look and you may find purple bell-shaped flowers growing from cracks all the way up the cliffs.

A long staircase climbs up the side of a particularly impressive cliff, then the trail levels off a bit as a view of Jordan Pond opens up. You then reach a rockslide, a jumble of large granite blocks that the trail travels over as it continues up the mountain. This section of rock-hopping requires some concentration as you judge the distances between rocks and decide on the best way to get through this rockslide.

After that, you'll reach one of the most intimidating sections of the trail, a fairly narrow area where the trail travels along the top of a cliff. While this section of the

An unusual wooden staircase was recently constructed on the trail

trail is plenty wide enough to hike safely, the dramatic drop-off to your right can be a bit daunting. Just don't forget to pause here and enjoy the view, which is wide open and extends all the way to the ocean. On a sunny day, you'll be able to see the different depths of Jordan Pond as the color of the water changes from turquoise to deep blue, as well as rocks shining in the shallows along the pond's edges.

The trail then dips back into the forest and climbs over the twisted roots of impressive white cedar trees. There in the woods, you'll come to your first section of iron rungs, which will help you get up and over a boulder. The trail then travels along the bottom of a cliff, descends a bit, and reaches a long metal rail that leads to an unusual wooden bridge-staircase. The trail then continues down, past a tiny rock cave, then back up again and along the top of a cliff once more.

As you're nearing the end of the trail, you'll come to the longest section of iron rungs, which form a ladder up the cliffs. Here you'll need to do a little hand-over-foot climbing, using the rungs as well as natural handholds in the granite. The view of Jordan Pond from this location is spectacular.

Soon after this difficult climb, you'll come to an intersection marked with a sign. Here you have a few options, depending on how long you want your hike to be and if you care about bagging a summit. Whatever you choose to do, it's advisable not to descend the Jordan Cliffs Trail, as descending steep trails is more dangerous than ascending them.

If you turn left at the intersection, it's 0.4 mile to the summit of Penobscot Mountain, and from there, you can descend the mountain on the Penobscot Mountain Trail for a loop hike that is about 3.7 miles long. Some people even add in the peak of Sargent Mountain and loop down to Jordan Pond for a hike that is 5.7 miles.

If you turn right at the intersection, you will be continuing on the final 0.2 mile of the Jordan Cliffs Trail. When it ends at the Deer Brook Trail, you can turn right and descend 0.3 mile (crossing a carriage road) to the Jordan Pond Path. There you'll turn right to hike an easy 1.5 miles back to Jordan Pond House for a hike that is 3.7 miles long.

It's important to keep in mind that the Jordan Cliffs Trail is usually closed in the spring and most of the summer because the cliffs are a nesting site for peregrine falcons. These birds are listed as endangered in Maine, and studies show that human proximity to their nests can result in nest abandonment. Typically, the trail is closed sometime in March, when the falcons arrive at the cliffs, and they reopen in early August, weeks after their offspring have successfully flown from the nest.

For more information: Call (207) 288-3338 or visit www.nps.gov/acad.

Personal note: We walked a mile in the wrong direction on August 8, 2017, and I blame Jordan Pond. It was just too beautiful to part from, with its crystal-clear waters, ruffled by a warm breeze and sparkling in the sun. My husband, Derek, and I had walked along the boardwalk of the Jordan Pond Path nearly to the pond's north end before we realized we were headed in the wrong direction to hike the Jordan Cliffs Trail. So after apologizing to Derek, I turned us around and we walked the beautiful, easy path back to the south end of the pond. At least our legs were warmed up for the hike, I told myself, though I dared not say it aloud.

From that point on, we looked at our detailed trail map probably more than necessary, double-checking that every turn was correct. Navigating the carriage roads and the Spring Trail, we made it to the Jordan Cliffs Trailhead just as a group of six young adults were also preparing to embark on the challenging hike. They had a dog with them, and though I dislike being a know-it-all, I voiced my concern that the dog wouldn't be able to hike the steep trail because of the iron rungs. They decided to try it anyway.

About halfway up the trail, as we approached the top of a cliff, I turned to see the dog off-leash trotting up behind us. I shooed it back, then told the group that they needed to put their dog on leash. A girl in the group replied that she didn't think her dog would jump off the cliff. I argued that she didn't know that—dogs do weird things. I watched as she put her dog on a leash. Feeling a bit better about the situation, I continued on with Derek.

As we crossed a narrow bridge and climbed the cliffs using granite holds and iron rungs, I wondered how the group behind us was doing. They had either slowed

Jordan Pond as seen from the Jordan Cliffs Trail

down considerably or finally decided to turn around. I hope they got down safely with their pup. We didn't see them for the rest of our hike.

Not one who is particularly afraid of heights, I truly enjoyed the trail, especially the steep sections where I could run my hands over the warm granite searching for handholds and footholds, then use them to hoist myself up onto iron rungs. Standing at the edge of the cliffs, with Jordan Pond and the lush forest far below, made me feel almost like I was flying, taking it all in from the wing.

As we neared the end of the Jordan Cliffs Trail, we turned left and hiked up to the top of Penobscot Mountain, then descended on the Penobscot Mountain Trail, which traces the mountain's bare ridgeline back down to Jordan Pond. The views along the way were so amazing that I had to force myself to stop taking photographs—and picking wild lowbush blueberries—or we'd never get off the mountain before dark.

Hike 19: Buck Cove Mountain in Acadia National Park in Winter Harbor

Difficulty: Moderate. The hike to the summit of Buck Cove Mountain is 4.4 miles out and back. Though the mountain's summit is 224 feet above sea level, that number is deceptive because the trail travels over a number of large hills on the way to the top. By the end of the hike, you will have climbed more than 1,000 feet. You can also lengthen the hike to about 6.5 miles by continuing south on the Buck Cove Mountain Trail to climb to the top of Schoodic Head, then backtracking to the trailhead.

Dogs: Permitted but must be kept on a leash no longer than 6 feet at all times

Cost: All visitors to Acadia are required to pay an entrance fee May through Oct. These fees vary in cost, with most visitors purchasing a vehicle pass for $25, which is good for 7 days. However, if you visit the park often, you may as well purchase an annual pass for $50. Park passes are available at several locations in and near the park, including park visitor centers. They can also be purchased online at www.nps.gov/acad.

Access: The trail is for foot traffic only and is open year-round. The parking lot is plowed.

Wheelchair accessibility: The trails were not constructed to be wheelchair accessible.

Hunting: Not permitted

Restrooms: Toilets are located near the day-use parking area near the entrance station.

How to get there: From the Route 1 bridge that spans the Mount Desert Narrows between the towns of Hancock and Sullivan, drive northeast on Route 1 through Sullivan and into Gouldsboro. Approximately 7.9 miles from the bridge, turn right onto Route 186 toward Winter Harbor. Drive 6.5 miles, then take a sharp left to stay on Route 186. Drive another 0.5 mile, then turn right onto Schoodic Loop Road at the sign for Acadia National Park. Drive a little less than a mile, then turn left at the sign for Schoodic Woods. Keep to the right to park in the day-use parking area.

From the day-use parking area, walk east to the large, stone information building. Continue east, following the main paved road past campground areas A and B to the group camping area at the end of the road, where you'll find the trailhead marked with a cedar post sign.

GPS coordinates: Parking area, 44.380312, -68.067426; trailhead at the campground, 44.381384, -68.058513

Rising 224 feet above sea level on the Schoodic Peninsula, Buck Cove Mountain is really just a hill, but don't let this deter you from considering it as a moderately challenging day hike. Located in Acadia National Park's only mainland section, Buck Cove Mountain can be reached on a blue-blazed hiking trail that travels through lovely cedar groves and wetlands, across bubbling brooks, and over several beautiful rocky hills covered with lichen, highbush blueberries, and twisted pine trees.

Running the length of the peninsula, the Buck Cove Mountain Trail is 3.2 miles long, making it the longest hiking trail in this section of the park. About 2.2 miles from the trailhead, the trail reaches the top of Buck Cove Mountain. From there, the trail continues south to climb to the top of Schoodic Head, the tallest point on the

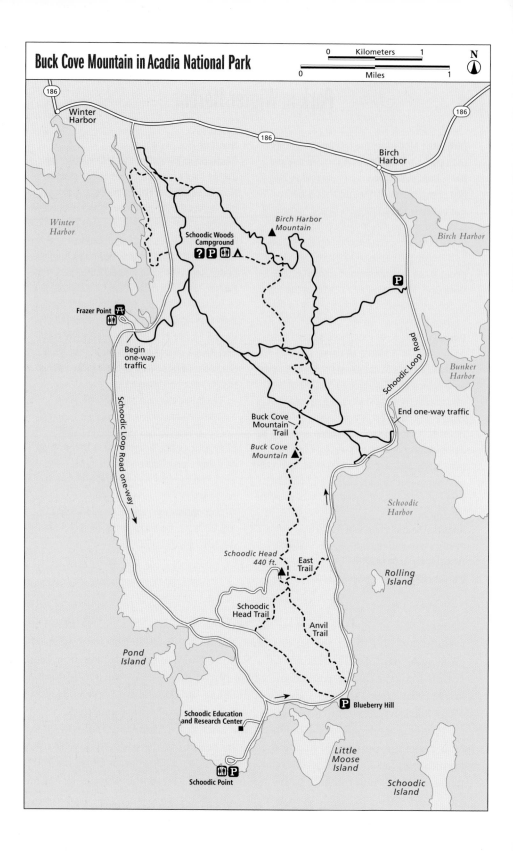

Buck Cove Mountain in Acadia National Park

0   Kilometers   1

0   Miles   1

N

186
Winter Harbor
186
Birch Harbor
186

Winter Harbor

Birch Harbor Mountain

Birch Harbor

Schoodic Woods Campground
? P 🚻 ⛺

Frazer Point 🏕
🚻

Begin one-way traffic

Schoodic Loop Road one-way

P

Schoodic Loop Road

End one-way traffic

Bunker Harbor

Buck Cove Mountain Trail

Buck Cove Mountain

Schoodic Harbor

Schoodic Head 440 ft.

East Trail

Rolling Island

Schoodic Head Trail

Anvil Trail

Pond Island

Schoodic Education and Research Center

Blueberry Hill
P

Little Moose Island

🚻 P
Schoodic Point

Schoodic Island

The ocean as seen through the trunks and branches of pines atop a hill visited by the Buck Cove Mountain Trail

peninsula at 440 feet above sea level. Regardless of whether you hike to the top of Buck Cove Mountain or continue past it to Schoodic Head, there are many interesting natural features to see along the trail.

Starting at the trailhead at the Schoodic Woods group camping area, the Buck Cove Mountain Trail climbs a gradual hill through a large stand of white cedar trees. The trail soon crosses a bike path two times, then visits a boggy area on narrow bog bridges. There you'll find cotton sedge and other interesting plants and mosses.

After passing a hollow tree full of mushrooms, the trail leads along the base of some dramatic cliffs, where it passes a tiny cave. The trail then heads uphill through an evergreen forest filled with mosses and lichens, crosses another bike path, then continues uphill through a forest of twisted pines, patches of bare bedrock, and low-lying vegetation. Atop this hill, at about 390 feet above sea level, you'll reach a fairly open view of the ocean.

Continuing south, the trail heads down the hill to a bike path, which is the lowest point in the hike at 78 feet above sea level. From there, the trail climbs to the summit of Buck Cove Mountain, which is covered with pine trees and offers only glimpses of the ocean and nearby Schoodic Head through the trees. The summit is marked with a wooden sign held up in a pile of rocks.

If you continue south on the trail from the summit of Buck Cove Mountain, you'll steeply descend the mountain, then climb up the gradual north slope of Schoodic Head. Atop Schoodic Head, which is covered in stunted jack pine trees, the trail

intersects with the 0.5-mile East Trail, 1.1-mile Anvil Trail, and 0.7-mile Schoodic Head Trail, all of which lead down to Schoodic Loop Road. While there are a few outlooks atop Schoodic Head, the Anvil Trail leads to a particularly good one atop a ledge, where you'll get stunning views of the ocean and Mount Desert Island, home to the much busier section of Acadia National Park.

Acadia National Park, Maine's only national park, is made up of several parcels. Most of the park is on Mount Desert Island, which is home to the park's most famous landmarks, including Cadillac Mountain, Thunder Hole, Sand Beach, and Jordan Pond. In 2016, as Acadia celebrated its 100th anniversary, the park saw an all-time record of 3.3 million visitors, and most of those were on Mount Desert Island.

Things are a bit quieter on Winter Harbor's Schoodic Peninsula, home to the park's only mainland section. In fact, it's a section of the park still in the process of being developed. To date, the Schoodic Peninsula features a 6-mile loop road with turnouts at views of lighthouses, the rocky shore, and cobblestone beaches; 8.3 miles of smooth, wide bike paths; and more than 8 miles of hiking trails. All of these trails are marked on the park trail map, posted at kiosks throughout the park and at the Schoodic Woods entrance station. In addition, the Schoodic Woods Campground opened in 2015, greatly expanding the possibilities for visitors. The campground includes individual and group camping areas, as well as RV sites.

Much of the Schoodic Peninsula used to be owned by John G. Moore, a Maine native and Wall Street financier. In the 1920s Moore's heirs donated the land—2,050 acres—to the Hancock County Trustees of Public Reservations, which in 1929 donated the land to the National Park Service to expand Acadia National Park.

In the 1930s and 1940s, some of this land was transferred to the US Navy to use as a radio communication station. The land was transferred back to the National Park Service in 2002, and the former naval base became the Schoodic Education and Research Center, one of 17 National Park Service research learning centers across the country. The center facilitates research projects throughout the park and hosts educational programs for visitors of all ages.

For more information: Visit www.nps.gov/acad or call (207) 288-3338.

Personal note: In September of 2015, I wrote a story for the BDN about the opening of the Schoodic Woods Campground, and in order to do that, I visited the park and walked around the campsites until I found several campers willing to talk to me about their experiences. Plants were still in pots along the side of the road, and the signs marking the new bike paths and hiking trails didn't have a scratch on them. I took the opportunity to briefly explore one of the new hiking trails along the water, but the sun was sinking fast and I was forced turn around before long. So I told myself I'd return to hike soon.

◀ *A tiny cave is found in a cliff beside the Buck Cove Mountain Trail.*

The fluffy tips of cotton sedge wave in the breeze beside a bog bridge on the trail in November.

Well, I didn't get back to the Schoodic Peninsula until more than a year later, on a crisp, sunny day in November. As my husband, Derek, and I walked through the campground with our dog, Oreo, we talked about how much fun it would be to plan a group camping trip there.

That day, we hiked the Buck Cove Mountain Trail, turning around at the summit of Buck Cove Mountain for an out-and-back hike of 4.4 miles. Along the way, we decided it was an especially good trail to hike in late fall because the forest was composed mostly of cedar, spruce, and pine trees, meaning it looks very much the same year-round, unlike deciduous forests, which tend to look bleak and colorless in November. We also decided it was a great trail for nature lovers because of the interesting variety of mushrooms and plants, including groups of carnivorous pitcher plants in a boggy area and a hollow tree full of small orange mushrooms.

About halfway through the hike, a cut that already existed on Oreo's foot opened up, but we were prepared with a first-aid kit. After cleaning his foot and squeezing a little antibiotic ointment on the cut, we wrapped it in gauze and athletic tape, and Oreo was good to go.

A highlight of the hike occurred while we took a snack break atop a hill north of Buck Cove Mountain. As we sat on a small rock shelf, a group of noisy red crossbills—a type of finch that can be found in mature carnivorous forests—flew to the top of a nearby spruce tree. At the time, I didn't know what species they were, but they caught my attention because some of them were orange-red, while others were yellow. I learned later that the orange birds are male and the yellow are female. I also learned that the tips of the bird's thick, curved beak cross each other in an odd way, and this actually allows the bird to access the seeds of cones. In all of the photos I took of these birds, they were doing just that, fattening up for the winter.

Red crossbills forage for seeds in the cones of a spruce tree by the trail.

Hike 20: Black Mountain Cliffs in Franklin

Difficulty: Moderate to strenuous. The Black Mountain Cliffs loop is about 3 miles long, and the side trail to the east peak, where you'll get the best views, adds another 2 miles to the trip, making the total hike about 5 miles. The trails on the mountain feature plenty of rocky sections and exposed tree roots, requiring hikers to watch their step. While steep in some places, these trails do not require hand-over-foot climbing. There are no ladders or rungs.

Dogs: Permitted on the trails and on nearby Schoodic Beach if kept under control at all times. Also permitted at the campsites at Schoodic Beach if kept on a leash no longer than 4 feet at all times.

Cost: None.

Access: The Black Mountain Cliffs loop is open for foot traffic only and is open year round. For campers, fires are permitted at authorized campsites or at a permit site with a permit from the Maine Forest Service. Campsites are first come, first serve, and campers can stay a limit of 14 days in any 45-day period. The road leading to the trailhead—Schoodic Beach Road—is not plowed in the winter.

Wheelchair accessibility: The trails were not constructed to be wheelchair accessible.

Hunting: Permitted. However, hunters are prohibited from discharging weapons within 300 feet of a picnic area, camping area, parking area, posted hiking trail, or other developed area. Loaded firearms are not permitted at campsites or on hiking trails.

Restrooms: An outhouse is located at the trailhead parking area.

How to get there: The trailhead for the Black Mountain Cliffs Trail is at the Schoodic Beach Parking Lot in the Donnell Pond Public Reserved Land unit. To get there from Route 1 in Sullivan, turn onto Route 183 (across from the Town Landing Road), drive 4.3 miles, and turn left onto the gravel Schoodic Beach Road. Drive 0.3 mile and veer left at the fork to stay on Schoodic Beach Road. Drive 1.9 mile to the Schoodic Beach Parking Lot at the end of the road. Start your hike at the far end of the parking area, past the kiosk, on the wide, smooth trail that leads to Schoodic Beach. A short distance down the trail, you'll cross a bridge and see the Black Mountain Cliffs Trail on your right, marked with blue blazes. Take that trail to start the loop hike.

GPS coordinates: The parking lot: 44.574027, -68.130030

Black Mountain rises 1,049 feet above sea level between two scenic bodies of water, Donnell Pond and Tunk Lake, in eastern Maine. A few hiking trails explore the mountain's exceptionally mossy forest and lead to the mountain's two peaks, which offer open views of the area.

Black Mountain is located within the state-owned Donnell Pond Public Reserved Land, more than 14,000 acres of remote forested land that features pristine lakes, secluded ponds, and a number of mountains in Hancock County. There are a number of great hikes on this property, and some are better known than others. Tunk Mountain, for example, is fairly well known, as is Schoodic Mountain. Black Mountain and its neighbor, Caribou Mountain, tend to see less foot traffic. And none of these mountain trails get anywhere near as crowded as the nearby trails of Acadia National Park on Mount Desert Island.

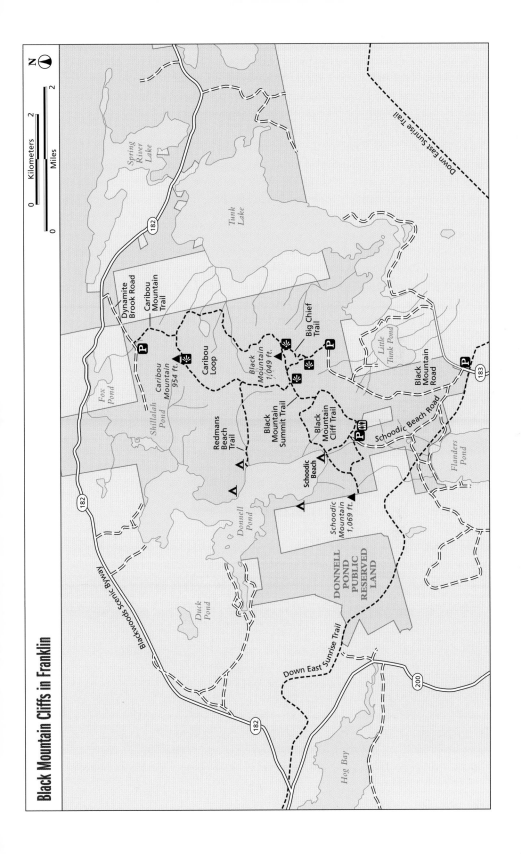

Black Mountain Cliffs in Franklin

Spring River Lake

Tunk Lake

Blackwoods Scenic Byway

182

182

Fox Pond

Shillalah Pond

Dynamite Brook Road

Caribou Mountain Trail

P

Caribou Mountain
954 ft.

Caribou Loop

Black Mountain
1,049 ft.

Big Chief Trail

P

Little Tunk Pond

Black Mountain Road

P

183

Redmans Beach Trail

Black Mountain Summit Trail

Black Mountain Cliff Trail

P

Schoodic Beach Road

Schoodic Beach

Flanders Pond

Duck Pond

Donnell Pond

Schoodic Mountain
1,069 ft.

DONNELL POND PUBLIC RESERVED LAND

Down East Sunrise Trail

182

200

Hog Bay

Down East Sunrise Trail

N

Kilometers
0   2

Miles
0   2

While I could describe a great many of the beautiful hiking trails in Donnell Pond Public Reserved Land, I chose Black Mountain Cliffs Trail because it seems to me to be the trail less traveled. Starting at a fairly busy parking lot at the end of Schoodic Beach Road, you begin the hike on the wide Schoodic Beach Trail.

Less than 0.1 mile from the parking lot, the Schoodic Beach Trail comes to the Black Mountain Cliffs Trail on the right, marked with blue blazes. At first, the trail climbs steeply through a hardwood forest, then levels out and crosses two old woods roads. The trail then starts to climb the steep southwest side of the mountain once more, becoming increasingly rocky and switchbacking up a few modest cliffs before leveling off again and striking through a couple of tranquil grass- and fern-filled clearings.

At 1.2 miles, the trail travels over the mountain's west peak, which provides limited views of the region. Near the peak, the trail comes to an intersection where you can turn left to continue the 3-mile loop and descend the mountain to Schoodic Beach Trail near Schoodic Beach. Or you can veer right onto Black Mountain Summit Trail and follow the signs for about 1 mile to the mountain's east peak, which is bald and provides amazing views of the region. While this 1-mile hike to the east

Plenty of signs, painted blazes, and cairns mark the Black Mountain Cliffs hike in Donnell Pond Public Reserved Land.

Oreo wades in the cool, clear waters of Donnell Pond, which lies at the bottom of Schoodic and Black mountains.

peak will lengthen your hike by 2 miles (out and back), the view is well worth the extra effort.

If you decide to take this lengthy side trip to the east peak, don't be thrown off when the trail starts to descend rather steeply. Looking at the map, you'll see that the trail dips down, then climbs back up again to reach the rocky east peak of the mountain. Along the way, you'll pass a trail leading north to Caribou Mountain, which is another good hike in the area.

After visiting the east peak and returning to the intersection on the Black Mountain Cliffs Trail, continue on the loop counterclockwise, heading northwest, then turning west to descend the mountain to Schoodic Beach Trail. There, you can turn right to walk to Schoodic Beach, which is a long, sandy beach located on 1138-acre Donnell Pond. Set back into the woods near the beach are several tent sites and outhouses.

From there, you simply follow the easy, 0.5-mile Schoodic Beach Trail gradually uphill to the parking area for a hike that is about 5 miles long.

For more information: Call Maine Bureau of Parks and Lands eastern office at (207) 941-4412 or visit maine.gov/donnellpond.

Personal note: I almost didn't make it out of the parking lot on July 1, in my attempt to hike Black Mountain Cliffs Trail. I simply couldn't find the trailhead. According to the trail map, the trail started on the east side of the parking lot. But it didn't. I found what I thought might be a trail, but it wasn't marked with blazes (as most trails are). Nevertheless, I followed the footpath up a steep hill and watched it quickly disappear. Meanwhile, my dog, Oreo was pulling on his leash, impatient for the adventure to begin.

Returning to the crowded parking lot in frustration, I inspected the trail map posted on the kiosk. Nearby, a beagle on a leash howled at Oreo, who barked back and yanked on his leash even harder. A deer fly circled my head; the sun beat down; the temperature rose above 80 degrees F; and my clothes started to stick to my sweaty skin.

Finally, I decided to wander down Schoodic Beach Trail, and lo and behold, there was Black Mountain Cliffs Trail, splitting off to my right. I was on my way.

That day, Oreo and I hiked the entire 3-mile loop, and in addition, we hiked over to the mountain's east peak, adding about 2 miles to the hike. The views from the east peak, even on that particularly hazy afternoon, were well worth the extra miles. Although Oreo and I passed a few people on the trail, we had the peak to ourselves. Sitting on the rough granite, we shared a pack of Smith's Log Smokehouse beef jerky, made in Monroe, Maine. We then headed back to the west side of the mountain and descended to Schoodic Beach, where Oreo went swimming and attempted to drink Donnell Pond dry.

Over the years, I've hiked a number of trails in Donnell Pond Public Reserved Land, which really is a hidden gem—a very large hidden gem. Just about an hour

Wildflowers rise above the clover beside the Black Mountain Trail in July.

Marked with blue painted blazes, the Black Mountain Cliffs Trail navigates around small rock cliffs as it travels up the mountain.

from my house, the state-owned property is home to a lot of great day hikes, and by now, I've walked nearly all of them. There are trails up Tunk, Tucker, Schoodic, Caribou, Catherine, and Black mountains, as well as an easier trail to remote ponds. And though I haven't planned a paddling trip there yet, I hear it's a great spot for that as well. Check it out. You won't be sorry.

Hike 21: Pigeon Hill in Steuben

Difficulty: Easy to moderate. The intersecting trails on the property together make up just under 2 miles of hiking. Expect a few steep, rocky sections, with the steepest section located on the Historic Trail near the mountain's summit, which is 317 feet above sea level.

Dogs: Permitted if kept on leash or under voice control at all times

Cost: None

Access: The preserve is open year-round from dawn until dusk. Fires, camping, ATVs, and snowmobiles are not permitted. The trails are for foot traffic only.

Wheelchair accessibility: The trails were not constructed to be wheelchair accessible.

Hunting: Permitted in accordance with state laws

Restrooms: None

How to get there: From Steuben, drive north on Route 1 about 4.3 miles from the Hancock-Washington County line. Turn right onto Pigeon Hill Road, then drive about 4.5 miles and park in the small parking area to your right, across from an old cemetery.

GPS coordinates: 44.454686, -67.883477

The highest point on the coast of Washington County, Pigeon Hill reaches just 317 feet above sea level, but from its top, hikers are rewarded with amazing views of the ocean. A small network of marked hiking trails explore the hill's rocky slopes and lead to its bald granite summit.

Pigeon Hill is located within the 170-acre Pigeon Hill Preserve, which was established in 2008 through the Summit, Forest, and Seacoast Campaign, a joint effort by the Downeast Coastal Conservancy and Maine Coast Heritage Trust to preserve Pigeon Hill, as well as Willard Point in Harrington and Tibbett Island in Addison.

From the preserve parking area, a trail travels into the woods and soon comes to a trail register, where hikers should sign in and pick up a preserve brochure. From there, the 0.3-mile Historic Trail, marked in blue, is to the left, and the 0.4-mile Silver Mine Trail, marked with yellow, is to the right. Both trails climb the mountain and have their own special features. The Historic Trail travels through a stand of jack pine trees, while the Silver Mine Trail visits the remnants of old silver mining activities that started on Pigeon Hill sometime after the Civil War. These remnants include piles of broken rocks, barbed wire fencing, a rocky access ramp, and a watering hole.

The Silver Mine Trail and Historic Trail come together below the summit at a big maple tree. From there, you can turn right onto the blue-blazed trail to climb steeply up the mountain for 0.1 mile to the summit; or you can turn left for a more gradual 0.3-mile hike to the summit on the yellow-blazed Summit Loop, which travels along lichen-covered ledges southwest of the summit.

Branching off the yellow-blazed Summit Loop are two additional trails in the network: the 0.6-mile Woods Ledges Loop, blazed in red, and the 0.1-mile Glacial

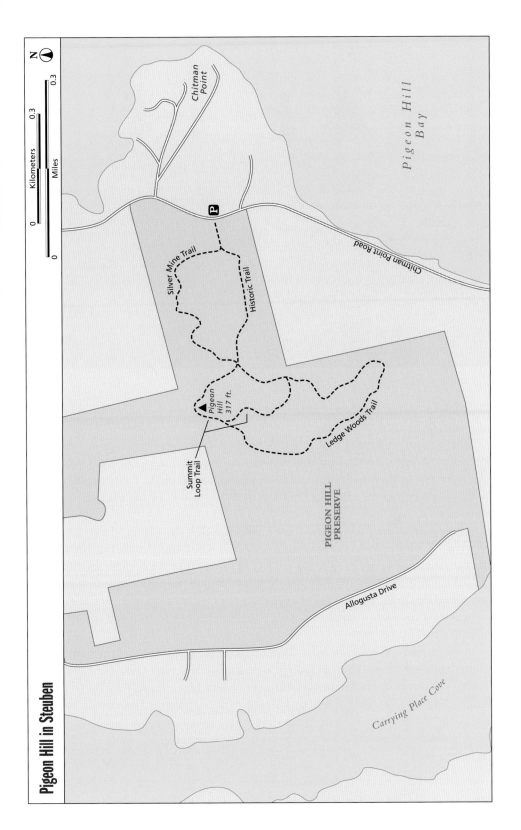

Pigeon Hill in Steuben

Chitman Point

Silver Mine Trail

Historic Trail

Pigeon Hill 317 ft.

Summit Loop Trail

Ledge Woods Trail

PIGEON HILL PRESERVE

Allogusta Drive

Chitman Point Road

Pigeon Hill Bay

Carrying Place Cove

N

Kilometers

Miles

0   0.3

0   0.3

The author and Oreo hike along the top of Pigeon Hill.

Erratic Spur, blazed in white. These trails explore the steep southern slope of the mountain. Signs mark the intersections in the trail network to aid you in navigation.

The summit of Pigeon Hill is clearly marked with a wooden sign in a rock pile. From there and several other outlooks atop the hill, hikers can enjoy unobstructed views of Pigeon Hill Bay and Little Bois Bubert Island to the south, Douglas Island Harbor to the east, and Dyer Bay and the small Carrying Place Cove to the southwest.

Also visible to the northwest of Pigeon Hill on a clear day is Petit Manan Island, which lies 2.5 miles offshore. Home to a stone lighthouse that's more than 100 feet tall, the 10-acre island is closed to the public and managed by the US Fish and Wildlife Service as part of the Petit Manan National Wildlife Refuge. It has long been considered one of the most important islands in the Gulf of Maine for colonial nesting seabirds. Nowadays it supports nesting by eight species of seabirds and waterfowl, including puffins and terns.

A few interesting natural features are marked on the preserve trail map displayed on the trailhead kiosk. They include jack pine woodlands visited by the Historic Trail, a big maple tree where the Historic and Silver Mine Trails meet below the summit, and ledges covered in lichen southwest of the summit on the 0.3-mile Summit Loop.

A maritime spruce-fir forest covers most of the preserve, according to a brochure provided by the Downeast Coastal Conservancy, though 10 additional plant

The trails exploring Pigeon Hill are especially rocky in some sections.

communities have been identified throughout the property. As for wildlife, birds are sighted year-round on the hill, including a variety of woodpeckers, grouse, chicka-dees, red-breasted nuthatches, dark-eyed juncos, American goldfinches, ravens, crows, and bald eagles. Deer, moose, black bears, and coyotes use the undeveloped part of the preserve, which is essentially the western half of it, and smaller mammals such as bobcats, foxes, porcupines, red squirrels, and snowshoe hares are fairly common.

For more information: Visit www.downeastcoastalconservancy.org or call (207) 255-4500.

Personal note: It was a warm Valentine's Day when I first hiked Pigeon Hill. The sun beat down, heating the forest to the 40s, but a thin layer of crusty snow still clung to the ground, and it crunched under my ice cleats as I hiked into the forest on the Historic Trail. As is typical in the winter, woodpeckers kept me company; they flew from tree to tree, searching for insects hidden in the bark. Deer tracks decorated the snowy trail, as well as other wildlife tracks I couldn't identify.

I hadn't expected the 317-foot-tall hill to feel so much like a mountain, with frozen lichens and low-lying plants scattered over its top, where I was rewarded with wide-open views of the ocean. The scene, with the bare granite and blue-berry bushes, reminded me of the tops of much larger mountains in nearby Acadia National Park.

Oreo looks down the Summit Loop Trail on Pigeon Hill in June.

Years later, at the height of summer, I returned to the mountain with my husband, Derek, and our dog, Oreo, and had a very similar experience despite the time that had passed and the change in seasons. Free of snow, the trails revealed themselves to be rockier than I imagined, and with leaves on the trees, the landscape was certainly more varied and colorful. But the stunning views were the same, and I could tell that Derek was pleasantly surprised, just as I had been when I first hiked up the hill.

Hike 22: Eagle Hill Institute Trails in Steuben

Difficulty: Easy to moderate. The trails travel through a mossy mixed forest that can be rocky and steep in some areas. Also, the land slopes downward steeply as it nears the rocky shore, offering a moderately challenging climb.

Dogs: Permitted if kept on leash or under voice control at all times

Cost: None

Access: The trail network is open to the public year-round during daylight hours and is for foot traffic only.

Wheelchair accessibility: The trails were not constructed to be wheelchair accessible.

Hunting: Not permitted

Restrooms: Visitors are welcome to use the restrooms in the Commons Building, which is open only during scheduled programs or courses.

How to get there: The trail network parking lots are located at the Eagle Hill Institute campus at the end of Eagle Hill Road in Steuben. From Route 1 (Main Street) in Steuben, head south on Dyer's Bay Road. Drive 2.3 miles, then continue on Modagor Road. Drive 1.2 miles,

then turn left onto Schooner Point Drive (there will be a sign at that intersection for Eagle Hill Institute). Drive about 0.2 mile, then turn right onto Eagle Hill Road. The campus is at the end of this short road, which is only about 0.2 mile long. Just after passing the Commons Building on your right, park in the gravel parking lot to your left.

There are four trailheads scattered throughout the campus for the trail network. I suggest starting on the Orchid Trail, which can be found by walking back to the campus road and continuing east just a few hundred feet. The trailhead will be on your left and marked with a sign that reads Orchid Trail. The trail leads toward the coast and intersects with many other trails in the network. Another good option is to start on the Leap Trail behind the Commons Building. This trail is the quickest route to the most scenic outlook in the trail network, Lover's Leap.

GPS coordinates: Parking lot, 44.459554, -67.933286

Located atop a wooded hill on the eastern coast of Maine, the Eagle Hill Institute campus blends into the densely forested landscape. Branching away from this quiet cluster of buildings is a network of about 2.5 miles of hiking trails that lead to blueberry fields, scenic overlooks of the ocean, a ridge covered with jack pines, and rocky beaches.

The narrow footpaths that make up the trail network at Eagle Hill Institute travel through a mixed forest composed mostly of spruce and fir trees, with a sprinkling of maples, birches, and other species. The forest also contains a variety of mosses, lichens, and mushrooms.

All trails in the network are named and marked with small square signs of different colors to help visitors navigate. For example, the Orchid Trail is marked with red squares, while the Bear Trail is marked with yellow squares that have a black slash through them. The Jack Pine trail is marked with purple, and the Blueberry Trail is marked with blue.

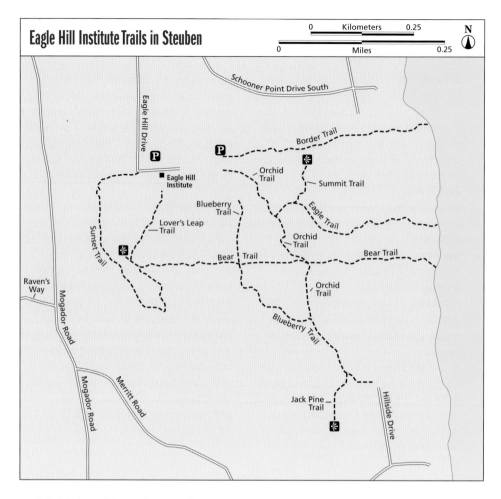

Highlights of the trail network include the scenic Lover's Leap and Grand Canyon Overlook, both of which provide partial views of the ocean over the trees; a blueberry field dotted with bird feeders; a stand of twisted jack pines on a rocky ridge; and three rocky beaches on the coast. The beaches have large blocky rocks that make great spots to sit and watch the rockweed sway in the salty waves.

Additional trails are in the process of being developed on the west side of the trail network near Lover's Leap. These new trails will explore three deep grooves in the landscape and will lead to an area in the forest that is filled with impressive boulders. Work on clearing these trails was under way in the fall of 2017.

Formerly the Humboldt Field Research Institute, Eagle Hill Institute is a nonprofit scientific and literary organization focused on serving scholarly and educational pursuits, especially in the natural sciences. At its campus on Dyer Point in Steuben, the institute offers seminars and workshops, as well as a residency program for

Derek and Oreo hike on a trail through the rocky woods of Eagle Hill Institute in late January.

scholars and scientific illustrators, the annual Northeast Natural History Conference, and public lecture programs.

A free trail map is available at the institute's main office, which is located just east of the Commons Building (the largest building on campus) and marked with a sign. The office is generally open 9 a.m. to 5 p.m. seven days a week, year-round. If no one is in the office, there is a number on the door that you can call for assistance from someone on the property.

For more information: Visit www.eaglehill.us or call the institute at (207) 546-2821.

Personal note: Not a speck of snow remained on the frozen ground of Dyer Point when my husband, Derek, and I arrived at Eagle Hill Institute with our dog, Oreo, in late January of 2017, to explore the institute's coastal trail network. The temperature, hovering in the upper 20s, seemed warmer when the sun escaped the fluffy clouds to shine down through the trees, but the salty sheets of ice we found on the rocky beaches reminded us that it was still winter.

In just a couple hours, we explored the majority of the trails, though we somehow missed Lover's Leap, which offers the best view in the network, according to Eagle Hill Institute director Joerg-Henner Lotze, who talked to me by phone after my visit. If you only have 30 minutes to explore the trails, he suggests taking the Leap Trail

Some of the trails at Eagle Hill Institute lead to the rocky shore in Steuben.

behind the Commons Building up to Lover's Leap, from which you can see across Gouldsboro Bay to Schoodic Head and the mountains of Mount Desert Island.

We started our hike on the Orchid Trail, which begins near the main parking area. Following the narrow footpath through a beautiful, quiet forest, we soon came to an intersection. From there, we took the Eagle Trail up a rocky hill to the Grand Canyon Overlook, which offered a limited view of the ocean. We then backtracked and took the Orchid Trail, descending steeply to the rocky shore.

We also walked the Bear Trail and Blueberry Trail that day, then hiked up to Jack Pine Ridge. Though there were many trails in the network, we didn't have trouble navigating thanks to the signage and color-coded trail markers. We kept Oreo on leash, and when I spotted a stand of trees with patches of bark recently stripped from them—a telltale sign of porcupines—I silently applauded our decision. I'm fairly certain we were the only people enjoying the trail network that day, but that doesn't surprise me. Few people think to explore the Maine coast during the winter.

Hike 23: Ingersoll Point Preserve in Addison

Difficulty: Easy to moderate. There are about 3.5 miles of intersecting trails in the preserve that travel through a hilly forest and along the coast. Expect exposed tree roots and uneven terrain. The Adler Woods Trail, which starts at the preserve parking area and strikes through the center of the preserve, is the easiest and most traveled trail.

Dogs: Permitted if kept on leash or under voice control at all times

Cost: None

Access: The preserve is open to the public for free year-round during daylight hours. The Downeast Coastal Conservancy asks that visitors stay on trail, avoid treading on moss, and respect the landscape. Fires, camping, ATVs, and snowmobiles are not permitted.

Wheelchair accessibility: The trails were not constructed to be wheelchair accessible.

Hunting: Permitted in accordance with state laws

Restrooms: None

How to get there: The parking lot for the preserve is at Union Church in South Addison. To get there from Route 1 in Columbia Falls, turn south onto Route 187 (Indian River Road) at Wild Blueberry Land. Drive about 1.5 miles, then turn left onto East Side Road. Follow East Side Road about 6 miles, then turn right onto Mooseneck Road. Drive 1.5 miles and Union Church will be on your left. Park in the back of the church parking lot, in front of the sign that reads Trail Parking. The trail leading into the network is to the right, marked by a preserve sign.

GPS coordinates: 44.512396, -67.715249

Located in the coastal town of Addison in eastern Maine, 145-acre Ingersoll Point Preserve features 3.5 miles of intersecting hiking trails that travel along the rocky shore and explore a beautiful forest filled with moss, lichen, boulders, and towering evergreens.

The preserve was acquired by the Downeast Coastal Conservancy in three parcels between 2009 and 2011, beginning with an 88.5-acre parcel that was donated by Dorothy Adler. In her honor, the main trail—a 1.3-mile path that travels through the center of the preserve—was named the Adler Woods Trail. The other two parcels that make up the preserve were acquired through Land for Maine's Future and North American Wetland Conservation Act funds.

With more than a mile of shoreline on Carrying Place Cove and Wohoa Bay, the preserve offers visitors plenty of opportunities to enjoy views of the ocean and observe coastal wildlife, including a variety of shorebirds and waterfowl.

Though the land has long been left wild, the 1861 and 1881 Washington County atlases show a homestead on the property with the name W. Ingersoll, and there is at least one cellar hole on the land near the eastern shore, surrounded by lilacs, according to the Downeast Coastal Conservancy. Bits of a stone foundation are also visible.

The preserve trail network consists of four trails, and each is marked with painted blazes of different colors. In addition, each trail intersection is marked with signs, and there is a trail map on display on the back of the sign at the trailhead. Preserve

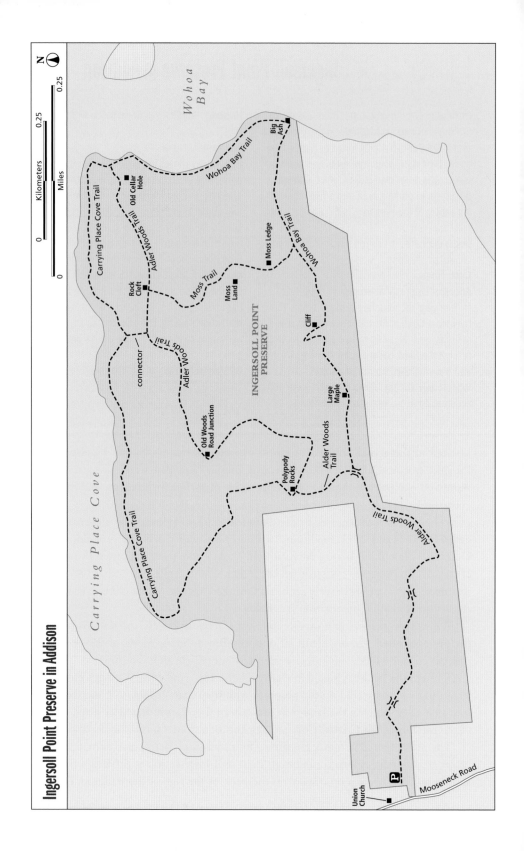

Ingersoll Point Preserve in Addison

The Cove Trail in Ingersoll Point Preserve is about 1 mile long, and much of it follows the shore along Carrying Place Cove.

brochures (that include trail maps) are available at the trailhead and at the registration box that is located beside the trail not far from the trailhead.

All visitors start on the Adler Woods Trail, which is marked with blue blazes and is 1.3 miles long, ending at the shore. Traveling through an incredibly mossy forest, this trail intersects with all the other trails in the network. It also passes the cellar hole of the Ingersoll homestead before ending at the beach at Ingersoll Point.

The Wohoa Bay Trail is 0.8 mile long and is marked with yellow blazes. This is the first trail to break away from the Adler Woods Trail. Traveling through the forest, this trail emerges from the forest onto a beach at Wohoa Bay, then traces the coast up to Ingersoll Point, where it reconnects to the Adler Woods Trail and the Cove Trail.

The Carrying Place Cove Trail, or simply Cove Trail, is about 1 mile long and is marked with red and pink blazes. The second trail to break away from the Adler Woods Trail, this trail starts at a big boulder known as Polypody Rock and heads north to the shore at Carrying Place Cove. From there, it follows the shoreline to Ingersoll Point, where it meets back up with the Adler Woods Trail and Wohoa Bay Trail. Along the way, there is also a cutoff trail back to the Adler Woods Trail.

And last of all, the Moss Trail is 0.3 mile long and blazed in green. This trail serves as a scenic connector between the Wohoa Bay Trail and Adler Woods Trail, passing through an area of the woods abundant in mosses and lichens.

The majority of the preserve is covered in what is known as a spruce-fir maritime forest, but two other forest types are present—spruce-fir cinnamon fern forest and spruce-larch wooded bog—according to the Downeast Coastal Conservancy. The preserve also contains two small shrubland areas filled with raspberry bushes, holly, wild roses, and meadowsweet. One shrubland area is near the trailhead, while the other is all the way across the preserve at Ingersoll Point.

The Downeast Coastal Conservancy is a nonprofit organization with the mission to conserve natural habitats and resources of the coastal watersheds, islands, and communities of Washington County. This organization was formed in 2009 through a merger of the Great Auk Land Trust and Quoddy Regional Land Trust.

For more information: Visit www.downeastcoastalconservancy.org, call (207) 255-4500, or email info@downeastcoastalconservancy.org.

Personal note: A storm was coming. Even if I hadn't watched the weather report like a hawk on December 29, 2016, I would have been able to feel it in the heavy air and see it in the dark clouds gathering overhead. As I drove east, it began to snow, then rain, then—to my delight—the rain stopped and I arrived at the trailhead of Ingersoll Point Preserve. On such a gloomy day, with clouds threatening to drop freezing rain

A dusting of snow can be seen on a footbridge on the Adler Woods Trail in late December.

Much of Ingersoll Point Preserve's forest floor is carpeted in thick moss.

at any moment, it didn't surprise me that mine was the only vehicle in the parking area. My dog, Oreo, and I had the preserve to ourselves that day, and we didn't mind that one bit.

As we followed the blue blazes of the Adler Woods Trail, the wind picked up, whipping through the treetops overhead, but in the forest of tall spruce, balsam fir, cedar, and pines, we were sheltered from the cold gusts. A dusting of snow covered the forest floor here and there, and a thin layer of ice had formed over pools. Icicles hung from boulders and frost clung to trees. But for the most part, the forest was filled with green, with a thick layer of moss covering the ground and creeping up tree trunks. Even on such an overcast day, it was one of the most beautiful forests I've ever seen.

That day, we left the Adler Woods Trail to hike the Cove Trail, which we followed along the coast to Ingersoll Point. Emerging from the forest at the scrubland at the point, I was taken aback by the fierce, freezing wind. It had also begun to drizzle. Clinging to a small tree at the edge of the shrubland, a hairy woodpecker braved the wind, the bright red streak on its head standing out against a gray world.

Oreo followed reluctantly as I walked onto the rocky beach to photograph mounds of seaweed, lichen-encrusted rocks, and the dark waves of Wohoa Bay. Shielding my camera lens from the rain, I took only a few photos and a video before running through the tall grass into the protection of the quiet woods. Oreo led the way.

Hike 24: Moosehorn National Wildlife Refuge Baring Division

Difficulty: Easy to moderate, depending on the trails and roads you choose to hike. The refuge features a wide variety of trails, including two wheelchair-accessible trails. For those looking for more of a challenge, there are several minimally maintained hiking trails that travel for miles through designated federal wilderness.

Dogs: Permitted if kept on leash

Cost: None

Access: The refuge is open to the public from half an hour before sunrise to half an hour after sunset, seven days a week, year-round. Bikes are permitted on certain roads and trails. Fishing is also permitted in certain areas.

Wheelchair accessibility: The refuge's 0.25-mile paved Woodcock Trail was constructed to be wheelchair accessible and travels through a forest that is home to the American woodcock, a bird that performs fascinating courtship flights in April and May. Moosehorn is also home to 50 miles of dirt roads that are closed to private vehicles and may be a good choice for wheelchair users looking to explore more of the refuge.

Hunting: Permitted with a signed Moosehorn hunting permit and appropriate state license

in some areas. Other areas of the refuge are closed to hunting. Permits and information about hunting areas and regulations can be acquired from the refuge office.

Restrooms: Toilets are located at the large paved parking lot just west of refuge headquarters on Headquarters Road.

How to get there: The Baring Division of the refuge is located in the town of Baring, which is just southwest of Calais in Washington County. From the intersection of Main Street and North Street in downtown Calais, drive west on North Street 3.3 miles (the road is also Route 1 and will become Baring Street), then turn left onto Charlotte Road. Charlotte Road leads through the refuge. As you follow the road, you'll come across a few trailheads and a wheelchair-accessible wildlife observation deck. Follow Charlotte Road 2.4 miles, then turn right onto Headquarters Road, which soon splits to become a one-way road that forms a loop and visits the refuge headquarters and a few different parking areas for various trailheads.

GPS coordinates: 45.115546, -67.278351

Established in 1937, Moosehorn National Wildlife Refuge covers nearly 30,000 acres in Washington County and is split into two divisions: the coastal Edmunds Division and the larger inland Baring Division, which is home to the refuge headquarters.

All national wildlife refuges, including Moosehorn, are managed by the US Fish and Wildlife Service (FWS), with the primary priority of protecting wildlife and its habitat, and a secondary priority of providing opportunities for wildlife-related education and recreation. Fortunately, these two goals often go hand in hand.

In the 20,000-acre Baring Division of the refuge, several well-maintained trails are located near the headquarters and information center. These trails include the 0.3-mile Woodcock Trail, which is a paved, wheelchair-accessible trail that is excellent for birding; the 1-mile Greg's Pond Trail, where hikers can enjoy wildlife watching

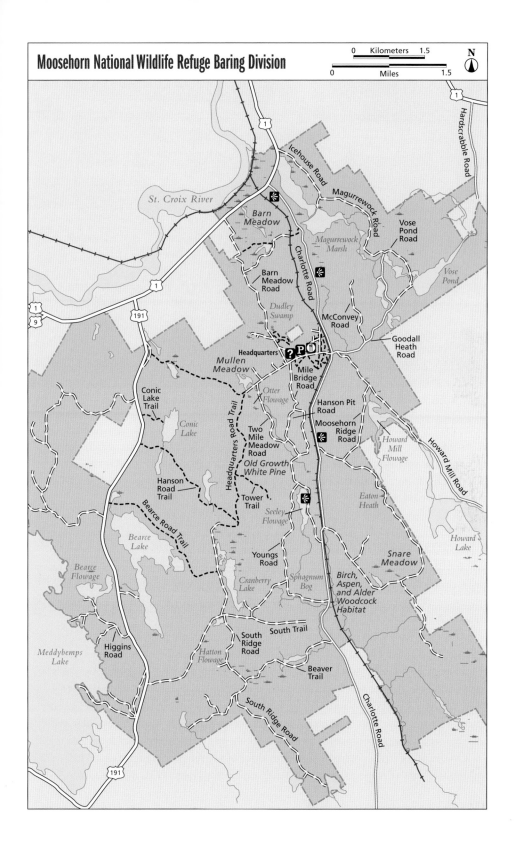

Moosehorn National Wildlife Refuge Baring Division

0 Kilometers 1.5
0 Miles 1.5

N

Lacey walks with her dog, Vail, on the 3-mile Headquarters Loop in May.

from an observation blind; the 0.7-mile Charlotte Trail, which is a paved, wheelchair-accessible trail with many interpretive panels; the 1.4-mile Raven Trail, which travels through a dense forest and fire break to Dudley Swamp; and the 3-mile Headquarters Loop Trail, an interpretive walk on dirt roads that visits several ponds and wetlands, as well as mixed forests and fields.

Along these trails are many examples of how FWS improves habitat for wildlife, with interpretive signs often nearby to explain the management practices. For example, Moosehorn's fire management program uses controlled burns to remove accumulated dead vegetation and minimize the chance of wildfires. FWS also conducts timber harvesting to clear areas of the forest and allow for new growth. These management practices create young forest where certain species thrive, including moose, deer, woodcock, and a variety of songbirds.

Also along the trails are examples of wetlands management, where water control structures on marshes and ponds allow managers to maintain optimal water levels for plant growth and feeding by waterfowl. The refuge is home to several wetlands, including a number of scenic ponds that serve as breeding areas and migration stops for a variety of waterfowl and wading birds. Black ducks, wood ducks, ring-necked ducks, Canada geese, and common loons are often spotted in the refuge's lakes and marshes, according to a brochure provided online and at the refuge headquarters.

On the other hand, approximately one-third of the refuge is designated as "federal wilderness" and is managed with a "hands-off" philosophy to allow these areas to develop into old-growth forests. In these areas, all mechanical means of transportation, including bicycling, are not allowed, but there are several primitive hiking trails that weave through these untouched forests for visitors to explore. Four of these trails—the Conic Road Trail, Conic Lake Trail, Hanson Road Trail, and Bearce Road Trail—have trailheads on Route 191 in Baring. Don't let the names of these hiking trails fool you; they are not like roads at all, but rather are narrow footpaths that are minimally maintained. In fact, refuge management advises hikers to bring a map and compass with them while exploring these trails because they can be difficult to follow at times.

Regardless of the trail or trails you explore, you're bound to see wildlife. Visitors often watch bald eagles and nesting ospreys off Charlotte Road, which leads through the center of the refuge to the headquarters. The birds can be viewed from a distance by using the free tower viewers at the large wheelchair-accessible observation deck off Charlotte Road.

The refuge is also home to a wide variety of songbirds, including 26 species of migrating warblers and northern forest species such as the boreal chickadee. Black bears are often spotted foraging along the refuge's many roads, especially in the

A great white pine stands out at the edge of a field beside a road that makes up part of the Headquarters Loop in the Barings Division of Moosehorn National Wildlife Refuge.

Woodland flowers called lady's slippers are in bloom in May beside one of the Mullen Meadow Wilderness Trails in the Barings Division of Moosehorn National Wildlife Refuge.

springtime and in the blueberry fields in August, according to refuge brochures. White-tailed deer, moose, coyotes, snowshoe hares, beavers, and river otters are also often seen.

For more information: Call (207) 454-7161 or visit www.fws.gov/refuge/Moose horn. The refuge headquarters, which houses the administrative offices, gift shop, and visitor information desk, is open 8 a.m. to 4:30 p.m. Mon through Fri. You can also find information on the refuge's mobile phone app at moosehorn.toursphere.com.

Personal note: A blanket of thick white clouds stretched to the horizon as I drove east on Route 9 with my friend Lacey and her dog, Vail, on a weekend in late May. But by some miracle, as we arrived in Calais, the sky cleared. Following Charlotte Road into the refuge, we pulled over to check out the wildlife observation deck, where we looked through tower viewers at an adult bald eagle perched atop a telephone pole overlooking Magurrewok Marsh.

At the refuge headquarters, apple trees scattered throughout the finely manicured lawns were in full bloom. As it was Sunday, the administration building was closed, but a refuge officer stopped her pickup truck and asked if we needed help. She then proceeded to let us into the administration building so we could snatch up a few brochures and a trail map, and when I asked her what the refuge's most popular trail was, she directed us to the 3-mile Headquarters Loop.

Glancing at a sheet on the desk, the officer reported that a young black bear had been spotted foraging by the refuge roads recently, but aside from that, the only reported wildlife sightings in the past week were lots of blackflies. So before Lacey and I headed into the woods, we sprayed on plenty of insect repellent, and even when we started to sweat in the sun, we kept our fleece jackets on. We decided we'd rather be hot than itchy.

Fortunately, on the wide Headquarters Loop, the blackflies weren't bad in several spots, especially where we caught a good breeze or entered an open, sunny area. Highlights of our hike were the scenic ponds located along the trail, where we spotted eastern painted turtles basking in the sun, waterbugs dancing over the still surface, dragonflies snatching up insects, and birds snatching up dragonflies. At one such pond, known as Otter Flowage, we sat in the grass and ate lunch while watching about a dozen Canada geese preening on the rocks and swimming through the perfect reflections of spruce trees lining the shore. In that one spot, the blackflies left us in peace—for the most part.

At one point along the loop, we became adventurous and veered off to explore the more primitive Mullen Meadow Wilderness Trails. We walked one of these narrow hiking trails for about 2 miles, stopping several times to admire different woodland flowers, including lady's slippers just blooming, patches of trout lilies, and violets. Finally, we decided to turn around at a fairly large pond, thinking that the hordes of blackflies—and occasional squadron of mosquitoes—just might drive us insane if we went any farther.

After our hike, we drove to nearby Calais, parked in the shade, generously cracked the windows, and left Vail sleeping in the car while we ate quesadillas and nachos at South of the Border restaurant, named thus for being just south of the US-Canada border and offering a wide variety of Mexican food, as well as a full bar and a menu of random comfort food such as hamburgers and chicken Alfredo. The prices were good, the service super friendly, and the food satisfying.

Hike 25: Little Mayberry Cove Trail in Grand Lake Stream

Difficulty: Easy to moderate. The trail is approximately 2.5 miles long and travels over many small hills. Expect a narrow but well-maintained path on fairly smooth forest floor with some exposed tree roots and rocky sections.

Dogs: Permitted if kept under control at all times

Cost: None

Access: The trail is open year-round during daylight hours and is for foot traffic only.

Wheelchair accessibility: The trail was not constructed to be wheelchair accessible.

Hunting: Permitted in accordance with state laws

Restrooms: Available at the boat launch parking area

How to get there: From the eastern Maine town of Princeton, drive north on Route 1 into the Indian Township Reservation, then turn left onto Grand Lake Stream Road and follow it for just over 10 miles. Turn right onto Little River Road and drive 0.1 mile, crossing the bridge over Grand Lake Stream, then turn right onto Shaw Street. Drive 0.1 mile to the boat launch parking lot, which will be on your right. Park there and continue north on Shaw Street on foot, passing the dam and boat launch and entering a neighborhood of camps along the shore of West Grand Lake. Along the way, you'll see signs directing you toward the Little Mayberry Cove Trail. Walk along this gravel camp road for about 0.25 mile to reach the trailhead, which is marked with plenty of signs.

GPS coordinates: 45.180674, -67.778271

Running through a mossy, hilly forest beside West Grand Lake, the 2.5-mile Little Mayberry Cove Trail is located in the 27,000-acre Farm Cove Community Forest, which is owned and maintained by the Downeast Lakes Land Trust. This quiet walk in the woods is punctuated by four outlooks along the shore of the scenic lake.

Founded in 2001, the Downeast Lakes Land Trust (DLLT) is a nonprofit organization that has purchased and conserved large tracts of forestland and shoreline in the Downeast Lakes Region over the past 15 years. One of the land trust's most recent accomplishments was its purchase of the 21,870-acre West Grand Lake Community Forest in 2016, which is adjacent to the Farm Cove Community Forest. Combined with other parcels of land trust acreage, it's collectively known as the Downeast Lakes Community Forest, totaling nearly 56,000 acres.

In addition to maintaining a number of hiking trails, DLLT manages nine water-access campsites on the Down East Water Trail, which provides a variety of options for multiday paddling trips in the region. DLLT also works with local clubs to maintain trails for ATVing and snowmobiling.

Designed specifically for hikers, the Little Mayberry Cove Trail was originally marked with yellow blazes painted on trees along the trail. However, those blazes have been replaced by tiny silver and blue signs with arrows pointing in the direction of the trail. In my opinion, these signs are more aesthetically pleasing than the bright

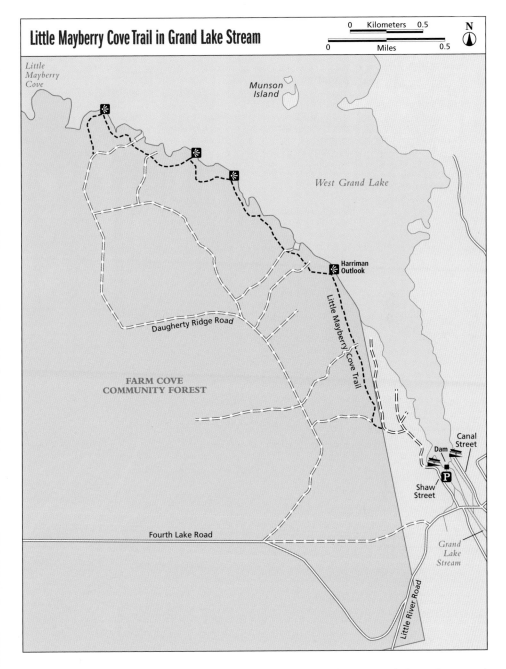

0   Kilometers   0.5

0   Miles   0.5

N

Little
Mayberry
Cove

Munson
Island

West Grand Lake

Harriman
Outlook

Daugherty Ridge Road

Little Mayberry Cove Trail

FARM COVE
COMMUNITY FOREST

Canal
Street

Dam

Shaw
Street

P

Fourth Lake Road

Grand
Lake
Stream

Little River Road

blazes. They're easy to spot, but at the same time don't detract much from the natural beauty of the forest.

Early in the trail you will come to a small wooden kiosk where hikers can sign a registration book and leave comments about their experiences on the trail. When

The farthest outlook from the trailhead on the Little Mayberry Cove Trail is at a peaceful cove on West Grand Lake.

you've completed your hike, this is a good place to offer any update on trail conditions, such as downed trees that need to be removed.

The trail travels through a beautiful forest that features hills of mosses and lichens, a wide variety of mushrooms, and stands of tall hemlocks and pines. In some areas the covering of soft, green moss is completely unbroken except for where boots have worn the moss down to dirt on the narrow trail. Be sure to stay on trail so as not to ruin this delicate natural carpet.

The first outlook on the trail is the Harriman Outlook, a tiny rocky beach that is reached by a short side trail. This is the only outlook on the trail that is named or marked with a sign. The other three outlooks are less obvious because they are simply areas where the main trail kisses the shore.

Just before reaching the far end of the trail, you'll come to the last outlook at a small, peaceful cove. There you can sit on small boulders surrounded by clear, shallow water and enjoy the view. Accessing the shore at this outlook may require bushwhacking through a little vegetation.

After the cove, the trail turns away from the lake to meet a logging road, where it ends. You can create a loop hike by following the logging road back to the boat launch, or you can opt to retrace your steps on the traditional hiking trail for an out-and-back hike that is about 5 miles long.

◀ *A thick carpet of moss lines the Little Mayberry Cove Trail.*

Silver and blue signs mark the Little Mayberry Cove Trail.

Other hiking trails in the area that are owned and maintained by the Downeast Lakes Land Trust include the 1-mile Wabassus Mountain Trail and the 0.25-mile Dawn Marie Beach Trail, both of which are out-and-back hikes. There's also the Pocumcus Lake Trail, which features two loop hikes, one that is 1.3 miles round-trip and one that is 3.6 miles.

For more information: Visit www.downeastlakes.org, call the land trust at (207) 796-2100, or email downeastlakes01@earthlink.net.

Personal note: When I drove to the secluded town of Grand Lake Stream in eastern Maine in late July of 2017, it was my first time visiting the area. I had read about the town, about its rich history as a place for fishing, canoeing, and hunting. But when it came to hiking, I wasn't sure what the area had to offer.

The Little Mayberry Cove Trail, easily accessible from the village, seemed a good place for any first-time visitor to start their explorations. As I walked to the trail from the public boat launch, I passed several families swimming in West Grand Lake, as well as people walking along the camp roads, but by the time my dog, Oreo, and I reached the hiking trail, we were alone. I scanned the registration book and saw that the trail was usually visited by few people each day, but it was by no means crowded. And on that particular day—a sunny Friday—we appeared to have the trail to ourselves.

Following the shiny metal trail markers, we entered a forest that became more mossy and beautiful the farther we hiked. At Harriman Outlook, I perched on a

Patches of sunlight illuminate the bright green moss that lines the trail.

rock on the shore while Oreo waded into the lake and thrashed about, barking and biting at the ripples and reflections—something he inexplicably does every time he's in water.

At the cove at the end of the trail, I sat on a rock, enjoying the sun and peaceful view of the lake. Meanwhile, Oreo splashed me as he smacked the crystal-clear water with his paws. We then turned back, opting to retrace our steps on the woodland trail rather than walk back on the logging road. When I return to the region, I plan to hike the land trust's Pocumcus Lake Trail and the nearby Wabassus Mountain Trail, both of which are maintained by the Downeast Lakes Land Trust.

Hike 26: Pleasant Pond Mountain near Caratunk

Difficulty: Moderate to strenuous. The hike is steep, leading to the mountain's summit at 2,447 feet above sea level in just 1.4 miles. Expect plenty of rocks and exposed tree roots.

Dogs: Permitted if kept under control at all times

Cost: None

Access: The trail is for foot traffic only and is open to hikers year-round; however, it may be difficult to access in the winter, as the road leading to the trailhead is plowed by a private landowner and the parking area is not plowed. Be sure not to block the road to traffic, as year-round residents live on this road.

Wheelchair accessibility: The trails were not constructed to be wheelchair accessible.

Hunting: Hunting is not allowed on the Appalachian Trail corridor, which sandwiches the trail and is about 1,000 feet in width. However, the trail goes through property where hunting is permitted. It's advisable to wear blaze orange during hunting seasons.

Restrooms: A new outhouse, constructed in 2016, is located at the Pleasant Pond Lean-to, which is approximately 0.4 mile into the hike.

How to get there: From the Caratunk town center just off Route 201, follow Pleasant Pond Road (opposite the post office) 3.2 miles to Pleasant Pond, then stay left at the fork onto North Shore Road. Drive 1.3 miles (with the road turning to gravel after 0.3 mile), then turn right onto a narrow gravel drive, which leads to the trailhead parking area in 0.1 mile. Appalachian Trail signs mark the drive and the trailhead, which is at the far end of the grass parking area.

GPS coordinates: 45.272785, -69.922055

In the rural northwest Maine towns of Caratunk and The Forks, the long ridge of Pleasant Pond Mountain rises to the east of Pleasant Pond, a deep pool known for its crystal-clear waters. As one of the many mountains traversed by the famous Appalachian Trail (AT), this mountain is enjoyed by hundreds of long-distance hikers every year. It also features a great day hike that leads to breathtaking views of the region from a number of ledges near the mountain's summit.

Starting at the parking area, hike northbound on the AT toward Pleasant Pond Mountain. The trail is fairly smooth, even, and flat for a stretch, giving you the opportunity to warm up your muscles before starting the steep climb up the northwest slope of the mountain. In fact, you'll actually travel a bit downhill on this section of the trail, through a mixed forest that includes a variety of hardwood and softwood trees.

About 0.3 mile into the hike, you'll come to a side trail on your right that leads to the Pleasant Pond Lean-to and privy in about 0.1 mile. This side trail is marked sparingly with blue blazes, while the entire AT is marked with telltale white blazes.

Continuing north on the AT, the trail becomes increasingly rocky and rough, with impressive tangles of exposed tree roots that make footing tricky in some areas. The trail also includes several long rock staircases, which must have taken trail builders a lot of time and effort to create.

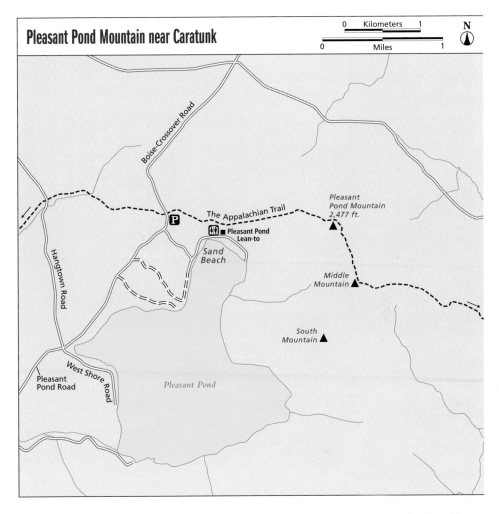

Near the summit of the mountain, the trail emerges from the trees all of a sudden to travel over an exposed stretch of bedrock dotted with stunted evergreen trees and patches of lichen and moss. The trail then dips back down into the woods briefly before climbing to the mountain's summit at 2,447 feet above sea level. Marked with a sign held up by a pile of rocks, the summit only offers a partial view of the region because of the surrounding evergreens. However, if you continue past the summit on the AT about 0.1 mile, you'll come across two outlooks that provide unobstructed views to the east and north, to the nearby cone of Mosquito Mountain and the long, glittering body of Moxie Pond. Beyond, the many peaks of the 100-Mile Wilderness and Moosehead Lake Region form a jagged, multilayered horizon.

From these outlooks, the AT continues north, descending to Middle Mountain and then down a long ridge to Moxie Pond, which is about 5 miles from the summit of Pleasant Pond Mountain. If just out for a day hike, I suggest turning around at the

Moxie Pond as seen from the top of Pleasant Pond Mountain in October during peak fall foliage season

second outlook atop Pleasant Pond Mountain, retracing your steps to the parking area for an out-and-back hike measuring about 3 miles.

The Appalachian Trail spans from Springer Mountain in Georgia to Katahdin in Maine, measuring approximately 2,190 miles from beginning to end. Thru-hiking the trail, hiking its entirety in 12 months or less, has become increasingly popular in recent years. In 2016, an all-time high of 1,110 hikers completed the trail.

In Maine, the AT is almost entirely maintained by Maine Appalachian Trail Club volunteers. Because of their efforts, the 281-mile stretch of the trail in Maine is almost always in great condition.

For more information: Visit www.matc.org or email info@matc.org.

Personal note: Though the Appalachian Trail is famous as a long-distance hiking trail, you don't have to spend months in the woods to walk this white-blazed portion of the path. Over the years, in an effort to complete day hikes on Maine's 281-mile section of the AT, I've studied maps and gotten lost plenty of times on logging roads. My trail explorations aren't always easy, but they're always worth the effort. The AT runs along some of Maine's finest mountains.

Colorful fall leaves litter the Appalachian Trail in early October on Pleasant Pond Mountain near Caratunk.

It was early October when I arrived in Caratunk for my first hike up Pleasant Pond Mountain, and I'll never forget the beauty of the fall foliage that day. The forests were a sea of vibrant reds, oranges, and yellows. That morning, I spent two hours with the AT ferryman, Greg Caruso, while he shuttled hikers across the Kennebec River by canoe. Caruso was kind enough to let me tag along so I could write a story for BDN Outdoors about his unusual job.

By the time I made it to the trailhead for Pleasant Pond Mountain, it was 11:30 a.m. and the sun was shining bright, filtering through the colorful canopy. Under a blue sky, the forest warmed to the low 70s as I made my way up the mountain solo, pausing to photograph particularly colorful leaves that had recently fallen to the ground and still held onto their vivid colors and interesting patterns.

Early in the hike, I spied a small garter snake, which slithered out of my way and then froze beside the trail, blending into the dead leaves. Other wildlife I observed on the mountain that day included a ruffed grouse (which many Mainers refer to as partridge), a hairy woodpecker, a red-breasted nuthatch, and plenty of curious red squirrels.

A sign marks the summit.

The author sits at an overlook atop Pleasant Pond Mountain in early October.

When I emerged from the trees near the summit of the mountain and paused to take in the first view, I was surprised by the emotions that welled up in me—a mixture of awe and joy. The landscape was on fire with fall color, and all I could see was wilderness—mountains, hills, ponds, and lakes, swallowing up any sign of civilization.

On my way up the mountain, I had run into only one other hiker, a woman who kindly shared her knowledge of the hike, instructing me to continue past the summit sign for a couple minutes to find the best views. I followed her instructions, finding two great outlooks atop cliffs on the east edge of the mountain's ridge. At both spots I lingered, enjoying the sun, the quiet, and the vast landscape.

Eventually, I turned around and made short work of the hike down. Then, on the way home, I stopped to buy a snack at Jimmy's Shop 'n Save in Bingham, where local businesses and some residents appeared to be in the thick of a friendly Halloween decoration contest. I don't think I've ever seen so many fake skeletons, spiderwebs, gravestones, and ghosts. And being a big Halloween fan, I was delighted.

Hike 27: Moxie Bald Mountain near The Forks

Difficulty: Moderate to strenuous. The distance of the hike varies from 4 miles to 13 miles, depending on which trailhead you start at and how much of the mountain's ridge you choose to explore. The trail is rocky and increasingly steep as it nears the mountain's summit at 2,629 feet above sea level. Also, several sections of the trail are crisscrossed with exposed tree roots, making footing a bit tricky.

Dogs: Permitted if kept under control at all times

Cost: None

Access: The trail is for foot traffic only and is open year-round; however, the parking lot is not plowed and sometimes Moxie Pond Road isn't plowed. The rough road to just above the Bald Mountain Brook Lean-to is not usually plowed.

Wheelchair accessibility: The trails were not constructed to be wheelchair accessible.

Hunting: Hunting is not allowed on the Appalachian Trail corridor, which sandwiches the trail and is about 1,000 feet in width. However, the trail goes through property where hunting is permitted. It's advisable to wear blaze orange during hunting seasons.

Restrooms: An outhouse is located at the Bald Mountain Brook Lean-to.

How to get there: There are two trailhead options for hiking Moxie Bald Mountain, and for both of them, the drive starts out the same. Starting at the intersection of Route 201 and Route 16 in Bingham, drive west on Route 16 for 5.4 miles, then turn left onto Town Line Road. Drive 2.6 miles to the end of the road, then turn right onto Deadwater Road. Drive about 4 miles to a fork in the road, then take the left fork onto Trestle Road, staying with the power lines. In 2.9 miles you'll reach an unmarked road on your right. This is where you decide which trailhead you are going to start at.

If you do not have a four-wheel drive vehicle, the only option is to continue straight on Trestle Road, which becomes Moxie Pond Road–Troutdale Road, for 1.8 miles to the parking area on your left. Cross the road to hike northbound on the Appalachian Trail (AT) toward Moxie Bald Mountain; the summit is in 4.8 miles.

For a trailhead that is closer to the summit, you'll need a high-clearance vehicle with four-wheel drive. The road has become increasingly rough in recent years, but trail maintainers continue to use it. Back at the intersection 2.9 miles down Trestle Road, turn right onto the unmarked road (which is just past an unmarked road on the left that has a bridge over Moxie Stream). Drive uphill 0.7 mile to a fork in the road, and take the left fork onto another unmarked road. Drive 3 miles to a bridge over Bald Mountain Brook, cross the bridge, and park on the right, well out of the way of traffic. Walk about 0.1 mile farther to where the AT crosses the road. Turn right to hike the AT northbound; the summit is in 2 miles. However, if you want to check out the Bald Brook Mountain Lean-to, it's just a short jaunt southbound on the AT.

GPS coordinates: Moxie Pond Road–Troutdale Road parking area, 45.249900, -69.830943; unmarked woods road parking area near Bald Mountain Brook Campsite, 45.258098, -69.796892

Rising 2,629 feet above sea level, Moxie Bald Mountain is one of the many peaks visited by the Appalachian National Scenic Trail, and it makes for a great day hike for people willing to navigate for miles on woods roads. The long, rocky ridge of Moxie

Moxie Bald Mountain near the Forks

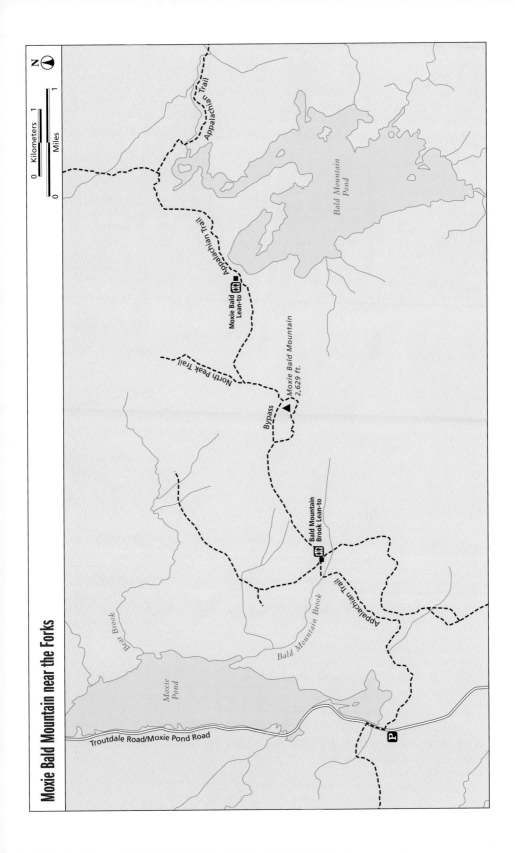

A woodland flower called painted trillium is one of the many species of plants that can be found along the Appalachian Trail on Moxie Bald Mountain.

Bald Mountain is above tree line, offering hikers unobstructed 360-degree views of the mountainous region.

Starting where the AT crosses Moxie Pond Road, which is also known as Trout-dale Road, you'll head north on the trail toward Moxie Bald Mountain and will soon have to ford (wade across) Baker Stream, which can be difficult during high water, namely in the spring or after a big rainstorm. The trail then gains elevation gradually. About 0.5 mile down the trail, you'll cross a power transmission right-of-way, and at about the 1.2-mile mark, you'll cross Joe's Hole Brook, the last water source on the hike. At 2.6 miles you'll come to Bald Mountain Brook Campsite near the crossing of Bald Brook, and at 2.8 miles you'll come to a 0.1-mile side trail that travels to the Bald Mountain Brook Lean-to.

Just after the side trail to the lean-to, the AT crosses an unnamed gravel road, which is the second trailhead option. From that point, the trail climbs through a rocky hardwood forest, which transitions to an evergreen stand, then becomes hardwood again before transitioning back to mostly evergreens. The trail becomes increasingly steep, passing a number of large boulders.

Before reaching the summit, you'll come to a trail intersection. If you veer left, you'll be taking the Summit Bypass Trail, which is 0.5 mile long and reconnects with the AT north of the summit. If you veer right, you'll remain on the AT and climb 0.3 mile to the summit. Along the way, the trail becomes even steeper and rockier,

Exposed tree roots crisscross the Appalachian Trail as it climbs Moxie Bald Mountain.

passing through a jumble of boulders that form a doorway and a couple of small, narrow caves. Near the summit, you'll break out of the woods and climb along a spine of bare granite following man-made directional rock piles known as cairns. The view from this spot is breathtaking.

Before reaching the summit, you'll come across a sign where you'll turn left to take a short side trail to the top of the mountain, which is marked with a sign surrounded by a pile of rocks. The summit is a wide-open space—hills of granite and stunted alpine plants. As you explore, avoid stepping on the delicate plants. There are great views in every direction.

To return, you can backtrack on the AT or take the Summit Bypass Trail back to the AT to make it a "lollipop" hike (a hike with a loop at the end). The Summit Bypass Trail passes some interesting landmarks, including a long, narrow granite ledge known as the Devil's Doorstep.

Another option is to continue northbound on the AT 0.6 mile to the 0.7-mile side trail to the North Peak of Moxie Bald Mountain. This hike is over open ledges and along a ridge that offers views in all directions. There are also a lot of lowbush blueberry plants along this section of trail.

The author and Oreo hike along the Appalachian Trail near the top of Moxie Bald Mountain in May.

Moxie, in addition to being a brand of soda, is a Native American word for "dark water." Throughout Maine, you'll find many mountains, towns, and bodies of water still hold their original Abenaki names.

For more information: Visit www.matc.org or email info@matc.org.

Personal note: The blackflies attacked as soon as we stepped out of the car. I'd expected as much. After coating myself and my dog, Oreo, with all-natural bug repellent, we set off at a brisk pace, attempting to leave the pesky flies in the dust of the old woods road.

Heading northbound on the AT, we waded through a bright green forest of beech and birch, pausing to inspect a cluster of large white tree mushrooms and photograph a woodland flower called painted trillium. But the insects were relentless, and I was forced to hurry onward to avoid being covered in itchy bug bites.

Oreo wasn't on leash, though I had one with me just in case he wandered out of sight or wouldn't listen to me. He must have known my plans because he was remarkably well behaved, running a bit ahead of me, then returning to my side as if to check on me, then running ahead once more—back and forth. He must have climbed the mountain 10 times that day.

As we gained elevation, the blackflies disappeared. The forest quickly transitioned to mostly evergreen trees and mossy boulders as we ascended the mountain. For a good stretch, I had to watch my feet lest I step in giant piles of moose poop. Oreo took a greater interest in a darker, smaller pile of scat, which I'm guessing was left by a bear or coyote.

The hike itself was well worth the long drive on rough gravel roads. We were up and down in less than four hours, and the views were fantastic. At the summit, Oreo and I sat and shared a bag of jerky and decided to continue north on the AT to the Summit Bypass Trail. By taking the bypass trail, we made a loop of the end of our hike, then backtracked to my white Subaru, Fred the Forester. It was sitting beside the old woods road, right where we left it, covered in blackflies.

Hike 28: Indian Mountain near Greenville

Difficulty: Moderate. The hike to the west vista near the summit of the mountain is about 3.4 miles out and back. The trail is steep in several areas, and the climb is fairly constant. Watch your step for rocks and exposed tree roots on the trail. You may also want to watch for piles of moose poop.

Dogs: Permitted if kept under control at all times

Cost: May through Oct, you must pay an entrance fee at Hedgehog Checkpoint on your way to the trailhead. Day use is $9 for Maine residents, $14 for nonresidents, and free for those younger than 15 years old or older than 69. The checkpoint operates from 6 a.m. to 9 p.m. daily. Passage is $20 per vehicle after hours. Camping is an additional fee. Checkpoints only accept cash or check. During the off-season, you may pass for free.

Access: The trail was constructed for foot traffic only. The woods roads leading to the trailhead are not plowed, so winter access can be tricky. One good option for hiking the mountain in the winter is to reserve a cabin at the nearby Appalachian Mountain Club (AMC) Little Lyford Wilderness Lodge. From the AMC winter parking lot, you must snowshoe or cross-country ski about 6.5 miles into Little Lyford. You could then snowshoe up Indian Mountain the following day, breaking up the adventure into manageable distances. The Indian Mountain trailhead is only about 0.5 mile from Little Lyford.

Wheelchair accessibility: The trails were not constructed to be wheelchair accessible.

Hunting: Permitted in accordance with state laws

Restrooms: None

How to get there: From the light at the center of Greenville, drive north on Lily Bay Road and turn onto the first road on your right, Pleasant Street. At 1.7 miles you'll come to an intersection, where you continue straight onto East Road. At 1.9 miles the road makes a sharp bend to the right, and it turns to gravel and becomes Ki Road. Several side roads branch off of this main road. Follow the directional signs to the AMC Little Lyford Wilderness Lodge, which is near the hike's trailhead. At 6.2 miles veer left at the fork in the road to stay on Ki Road. At around the 12-mile mark, you'll reach Hedgehog Gate, where you'll need to pay a fee. Past Hedgehog Gate, continue 1.9 miles and turn left onto Upper Valley Road. Reset your odometer and drive 2.3 miles to the first trailhead to Indian Mountain on the left; or continue another 0.2 mile to the second trailhead, also on the left. A trail leaves from both trailheads, and they come together 0.4 mile up the mountain.

GPS coordinates: 45.517289, -69.365357

Indian Mountain rises 2,341 feet above sea level in the Appalachian Mountain Club Recreation and Conservation Area, an expanse of wilderness east of Moosehead Lake that is accessible only by gravel woods roads. A hiking trail called the Laurie's Ledge Trail leads to two outlooks near the top of the mountain that offer two entirely different views of the region.

To reach the Laurie's Ledge Trail, hikers have two trailhead options on Upper Valley Road near the entrance of Little Lyford Lodge. A trail starts at each of these trailheads, and these two trails climb the mountain gradually to intersect at 0.4 mile. From

Indian Mountain near Greenville

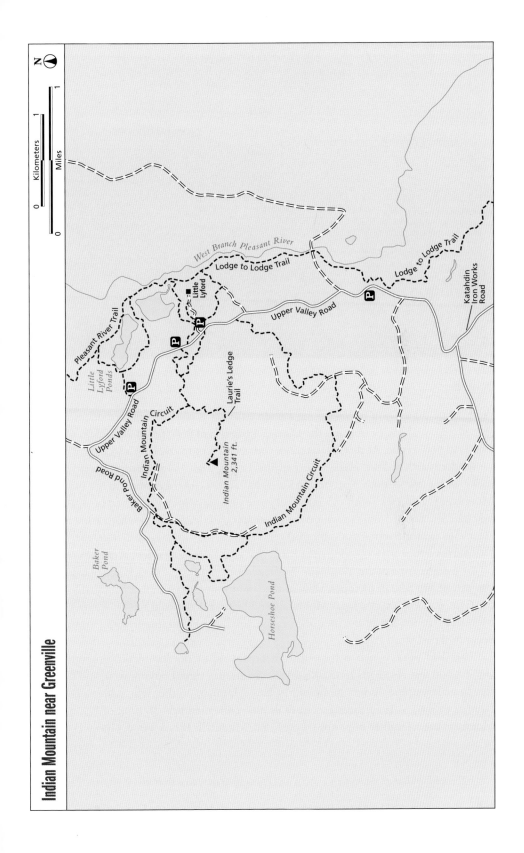

N

Kilometers
0   1

Miles
0   1

West Branch Pleasant River

Lodge to Lodge Trail

Lodge to Lodge Trail

Little Lyford

Upper Valley Road

Katahdin
Iron Works
Road

Pleasant River Trail

Little
Lyford
Ponds

Laurie's Ledge Trail

Indian Mountain Circuit

Indian Mountain
2,341 ft.

Indian Mountain Circuit

Upper Valley Road

Baker Pond Road

Baker
Pond

Horseshoe Pond

The Little Lyford Ponds and the Gulf Hagas–White Cap Mountain range as seen from Indian Mountain

there, a sign directs you to hike along a wide trail that is marked with red diamond-shaped signs and blazes to reach the Laurie's Ledge Trail and Indian Mountain Circuit Trail in 0.3 mile. At that intersection, you veer left onto the Laurie's Ledge Trail.

Marked with yellow blazes, the Laurie's Ledge Trail is increasingly steep and rocky, with a few sections of stone and log steps. From its intersection with the Indian Mountain Circuit, it's about 0.5 mile to Laurie's Ledge, which is reached by a short side trail, and about 1 mile to where the mountain trail dead-ends at what's known as West Vista near the mountain's summit.

Laurie's Ledge is an opening on a ledge that is just over 2,000 feet above sea level on the eastern slope of the mountain. At the outlook is a small wooden bench, where you can sit and take in the open view of the land to the east of Indian Mountain. To the right, you'll see Gulf Hagas Mountain, and behind it, the bald top of White Cap Mountain. To the left of the mountain range, you'll see First Little Lyford Pond and Second Little Lyford Pond.

The West Vista, which is located a bit northwest of the mountain's summit at about 2,300 feet above sea level, also offers an amazing view. Looking west, you'll be able to make out the distinct bump of Elephant Mountain to the right, where a B-52 bomber crashed in 1963, killing seven of its nine crew members. In front of Elephant Mountain are a number of ponds—Lost Pond, Mountain Brook Pond, Grassy Pond,

The trail up Indian Mountain is steep and crisscrossed with tree roots above Laurie's Ledge. ▶

Horseshoe Pond, Pearl Ponds, and Blue Ridge as seen from a viewpoint near the summit

and Pearl Pond—and to the left of the mountain is Horseshoe Pond and the Blue Ridge range.

For more information: Visit www.outdoors.org, call (207) 695-3085, or visit the AMC office at 15 Moosehead Lake Rd. in Greenville.

Personal note: The grassy patch that served as a parking area for the Indian Mountain trails was empty on July 3, 2015, when I arrived with my dog, Oreo, to hike to the outlooks on the mountain. I wasn't surprised. The man collecting fees at Hedgehog Gate had told me that few people pass through the gate with the sole intention of hiking Indian Mountain. Most day hikers are headed to nearby Gulf Hagas.

Mosquitoes and deerflies homed in on Oreo and me as soon as we stepped out of the car, so I rubbed all-natural bug repellent on both of us before gathering our gear and changing into my hiking boots. As I stuffed sweating water bottles into my pack, an all-terrain vehicle pulled up and the passenger, a young woman, dismounted. She thanked the driver for the lift and he sped off, back down the dusty road. She was hiking the mountain, too, she told me. We chatted about the fine weather, then she hit the trail. I waited a few minutes before entering the woods myself. I didn't want to crowd her.

After the long, bumpy car ride, Oreo was eager to get going—but when isn't he? Straining at the end of his leash, he pulled me up the narrow trail. I battled with him for a while, and eventually he calmed down.

It was almost a constant climb, and soon enough, the 70-degree weather felt more like 80. Along the way, Oreo pounced on something beside the trail. Worried he'd harm a wild animal, I yanked him back with his leash, and as I was doing so, a large toad jumped up and smacked him in the nose. I swear I could read the confusion in Oreo's face. Gripping his leash tightly, I laughed as I watched the toad disappear into the underbrush.

At Laurie's Ledge, we met up with the hiker we'd seen at the trailhead. She seemed open to talking, so I sat and we had a little conversation—first about the trail, then about ourselves. She used to live in Tennessee and had quit her job as a cardiac specialist to move to Maine and work at the Appalachian Mountain Club's Little Lyford Wilderness Lodge for the summer. She'd arrived just six days before, and as a staff member at the lodge, it was her job to know about the area's recreational opportunities so she could pass that knowledge along to guests. She had been spending the past few days paddling and hiking, she said, and it was a blast.

She didn't plan on hiking all the way to the West Vista that day, she said. Maybe some other time. Her goal was to hike Katahdin—Maine's tallest mountain—by the end of the summer. I told her a bit about Katahdin, then left her to enjoy the view at Laurie's Ledge.

Crisscrossed with tangles of exposed tree roots, the steep climb to the West Vista was well worth the effort. I sat there on the ledge, enjoying spectacular views as a strong wind battered my sweaty T-shirt, cooling me down after the steady climb.

Sometimes when I'm atop a mountain like that, I wish I could just soar down, riding the thermals like a turkey vulture. But instead, I have half a hike ahead of me. And while I find the ascent to be more difficult, it's on the descent that most people slip and injure themselves. Maybe it's because they're tired from the climb, or maybe it has something to do with it technically being more difficult to walk downhill than uphill. That day, I blame Oreo for my downhill tumble. It was likely a squirrel that caused him to bolt, but I'll never be sure because as soon as he yanked on his leash, my boot slipped on a tree root and down I went, sliding down the hill to rest in a pile of fairly fresh moose poop. After inspecting the long scrape on my leg and blossoming bruise on my forearm, I slowly stood up and dusted myself off. Oreo turned around and looked at me sheepishly. I just shook my head and continued down the mountain.

Hike 29: Little Kineo Mountain in Days Academy Grant Township

Difficulty: Moderate. The hike is fairly short—between 1.5 and 2 miles round-trip, depending on how far along the ridge you want to explore—but it's extremely rocky and includes several steep sections.

Dogs: Permitted if kept under control at all times

Cost: None

Access: The trail is for foot traffic only. Fires are not permitted. During the winter, the miles of logging roads leading up to the trailhead are not usually plowed; however, the roads can be traveled by snowmobile.

Wheelchair accessibility: The trails were not constructed to be wheelchair accessible.

Hunting: Permitted in accordance with state laws

Restrooms: None

How to get there: Starting at the light at the center of Greenville, turn onto Lily Bay Road, traveling along the east side of Moosehead Lake, which will be on your left. Drive approximately 18.5 miles to Kokadjo Trading Post and Camps on First Roach Pond. This is your last opportunity to purchase supplies. Reset your odometer. Continue on the main road 0.3 mile, and turn left onto Silas Hill Road just after the pavement ends. At 1.5 miles turn left onto Spencer Bay Road. At 1.9 miles you'll cross a bridge over Lazy Tom Stream. (There are many small side roads. Stay straight on the main road.) At 9.9 miles you'll cross a bridge over Spencer Stream, and to your right will be Spencer Pond and a great view of Little Spencer Mountain. Continue and at 11.8 miles you'll come to a fork; veer right to stay on the main road. At 13.7 miles you'll cross a narrow bridge over Lucky Brook, and at 15.5 miles you'll cross a bridge over Cowan Brook. At 15.6 miles you'll come to a major intersection where you'll turn right. At 15.9 miles you'll see a side road on the right with a bridge; stay straight on the main road. At 16.3 miles you'll come to a fork in the road; veer left to stay on the main road. At 16.8 miles you'll come to a side road on your left; veer right to stay on the main road. At 17.4 mile there will be a side road to your right; keep straight on main road. Finally, at 17.8 miles turn into the small trailhead parking area on your right. It's marked with a small sign and a kiosk.

GPS coordinates: 45.730534, -69.687543

Mount Kineo, with its dramatic cliffs, is arguably the most famous mountain in the Moosehead Lake Region. Located on a peninsula at the center of Moosehead Lake, Mount Kineo is topped with a large observation tower that many hikers climb each season. Little Kineo Mountain, on the other hand, is seldom talked about. Tucked in the forest northeast of Kineo, it too offers a rewarding hike that culminates in spectacular views of the region. And despite the implications of its name, Little Kineo Mountain is actually 137 feet taller than the famous Kineo.

Rising 1,926 feet above sea level east of Moosehead Lake, Little Kineo Mountain is located on state-owned public reserved land and features a blazed hiking trail that is about 1 mile long and maintained by the Maine Bureau of Parks and Lands. This

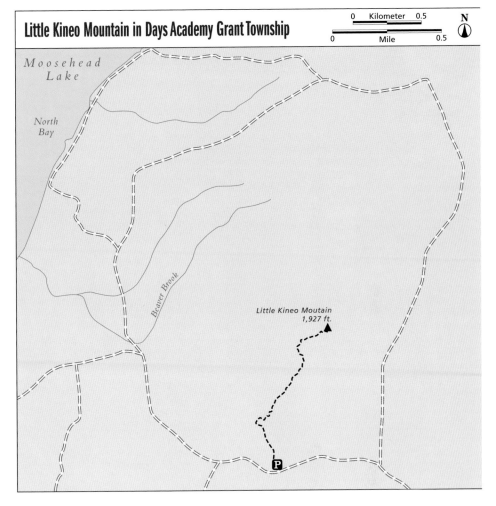

0   Kilometer   0.5

0   Mile   0.5

N

Moosehead Lake

North Bay

Beaver Brook

Little Kineo Moutain
1,927 ft.

P

trail can only be reached by navigating a confusing network of logging roads, making this hike feel especially remote.

Marked with blue blazes and cairns (rock piles), the Little Kineo Mountain Trail starts out in mixed forest that includes many yellow and paper birch trees as it approaches the mountain's south slope, then starts to climb. As the trail nears the top of the mountain, it becomes increasingly rocky and steep. These rocks can be very sharp, so be sure to wear sturdy hiking boots with good rubber soles, and if you're hiking with a dog, check its paws from time to time for cuts. Medical tape is a great way to protect a cut until you get off the mountain.

The mountain's peak, on the south end of the ridge, is marked with a large rock cairn on bare bedrock. From that point, you will have a partial 360-degree view over the tops of evergreen trees that surround the summit. But if you continue on the trail past the summit, exploring the mountain's rocky ridge, you'll come to an open ledge

A sign posted high on a white birch tree marks the trailhead for the hiking trail.

with unobstructed views to the west to Moosehead Lake, Mount Kineo, and across the lake to Big Moose Mountain.

From there, the trail continues on, dipping down into the forest, then climbing up a steep rocky slope to dead-end on the rocky high point on the north end of the ridge. This outlook offers a view to the northeast, which includes Big Spencer and Little Spencer mountains, and on a clear day, you'll be able to make out Katahdin—Maine's tallest mountain—in the distance.

For more information: Call the Maine Bureau of Parks and Lands western office in Farmington at (207) 778-8231.

Personal note: On a Sunday in mid-November, under a ceiling of thick white clouds, we navigated the web of logging roads east of Moosehead Lake.

"The weather report called for sunny skies," I told my husband, Derek, trying to sound optimistic. "Maybe it will clear up."

It didn't. But the clouds lifted high enough in the sky to allow us partial views from the top of Little Kineo Mountain, and as we hiked along the ridge, we excitedly noticed that tiny snowflakes were floating down to melt on our flushed cheeks. It was our first snow of the year.

◄ *Derek hikes down a rocky section of the trail on Little Kineo Mountain.*

Big Moose Mountain and small islands in Moosehead Lake as seen from a viewpoint on the south side of Little Kineo Mountain

For our dog, Oreo, it's all about the ice. Near the summit, we stopped for a break and let Oreo lick the icy surface of a small pool in the bedrock. Then Derek got him all worked up, and before long, Oreo was biting and digging at the ice with gusto, making both of us laugh.

While the weather wasn't perfect for seeing far into the distance, the views we did get were impressive. I can only imagine how many more peaks we could have seen on a clear day.

Hike 30: Lobster Mountain in Lobster Township

Difficulty: Strenuous. This adventure requires a total of 4 miles of hiking and 3 to 4 miles of paddling. The hiking trail leading up Lobster Mountain is steep and rocky in some areas, but it does not require any hand-over-foot climbing and does not feature any ladders, rungs, or ropes.

Dogs: Permitted if kept under control at all times. While dogs do not need to be on leash on the trail, they must be leashed and attended if staying at a campsite.

Cost: $10 per person, paid at the Caribou Checkpoint on Golden Road before reaching the boat launch

Access: There are no roads leading directly to the trail. It is only accessible by water, so the hike will require extra planning and equipment. The 13 campsites on Lobster Lake are also only accessible by water. Campers may not exceed a 14-day stay in a 45-day period, and campsites are first come, first served.

Wheelchair accessibility: The trails were not constructed to be wheelchair accessible.

Hunting: Permitted; however, loaded firearms are not permitted at campsites or on hiking trails, and visitors cannot discharge any weapons within 300 feet of a picnic, camping, or parking area; posted hiking trail; or other developed area (such as a boat launch). Bear baiting is by permit only.

Restrooms: There is an outhouse at the Lobster Stream boat launch at the beginning of your journey and outhouses for each of the 13 campsites on Lobster Lake.

How to get there: Just a warning: This adventure is far from any towns. Plan on driving on well-maintained logging roads for several miles. To navigate, it's best to use an up-to-date DeLorme *Maine Atlas & Gazetteer.* I advise against trusting a GPS device for this trip.

From the traffic light in downtown Greenville, take Lily Bay Road and drive along the east side of Moosehead Lake. In 18.5 miles you'll reach Kokadjo village, where you'll find the Kokadjo Trading Post and Convenience Store. Reset your odometer. Continue past the store and in 0.3 mile, right after the road turns from pavement to gravel, veer left at the fork onto Sias Hill Road. The idea is to stay on Sias Hill Road all the way to Golden Road. Along the way, ignore small side roads shooting off in every direction. Sias Hill Road is the main road and noticeably wider and better maintained. About 4.3 miles from the store, you'll reach a major fork in the road; veer right to remain on Sias Hill Road. At 6.8 miles you'll reach another major intersection; veer right to remain on Sias Hill Road. At 8.1 mile Bear Brook Road will branch off on your left; ignore it. At 14.6 miles you'll meet Golden Road; turn left. Reset your odometer and drive on the wide, gravel Golden Road, passing Caribou Lake on your right. At 6.2 miles you'll come to Caribou Checkpoint, where you'll need to pay a fee to pass through the gate and spend the day. About 9 miles from the gate, turn left onto Lobster Trip Road and drive 3.5 miles, cross a bridge over Lobster Stream, and turn left into the boat launch parking lot.

GPS coordinates: 45.892226, -69.564687

Lobster Mountain, rising 2,318 feet above sea level by scenic Lobster Lake, is a hiking destination for the truly adventurous. Reachable only by boat, the hiking trail that leads up Lobster Mountain is about 2 miles long, ending at a scenic outcrop near the mountain's wooded summit.

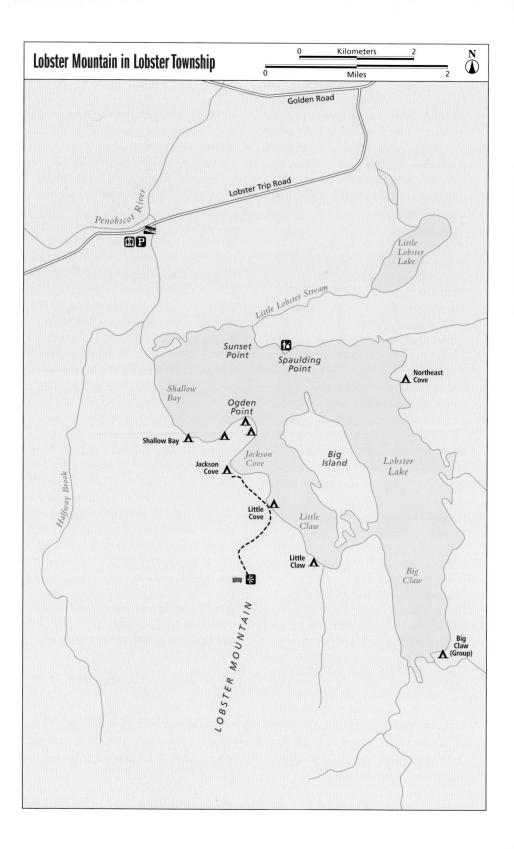

Lobster Mountain in Lobster Township

0   Kilometers   2

0   Miles   2

N

Golden Road

Lobster Trip Road

Penobscot River

Little Lobster Stream

Little Lobster Lake

Sunset Point

Spaulding Point

Northeast Cove

Shallow Bay

Ogden Point

Shallow Bay

Jackson Cove

Big Island

Lobster Lake

Halfway Brook

Jackson Cove

Little Cove

Little Claw

Little Claw

Big Claw

Big Claw (Group)

LOBSTER MOUNTAIN

Lobster Mountain as seen from Lobster Lake. Campsites are located along the shore of the lake, and a 2-mile hiking trail leads to the top of the mountain.

Just getting to the trailhead for the hike is a challenge that requires navigating miles of logging roads and paddling up Lobster Stream and across the northern part of Lobster Lake. The stream, lake, and mountain are all on state-owned land as part of the Penobscot River Corridor, which is also a section of the Northern Forest Canoe Trail, a historic 740-mile water trail through New York, Vermont, Quebec, New Hampshire, and Maine.

Starting at the public boat launch on Lobster Stream, you'll paddle upstream (south) a little over 1 mile to Lobster Lake. The stream is an easy paddle, with slow-moving water. Spruce trees line the shore, and near the mouth of the stream, you'll pass a beaver lodge and wetlands that moose and other wildlife frequent.

Once at Lobster Lake, the quickest way to the trailhead is by striking southeast, toward the tip of Ogden Point. However, if the water is choppy, you may want to veer right (south) and trace the shore for a longer but safer paddle. Along the way you'll pass a sandy beach, and as you paddle out and around Ogden Point, you'll see several campsites that are open to the public on a first-come, first-served basis.

Paddling around Ogden Point, you'll enter a small cove. The trailhead is across the cove, at its south end, and is marked with a brown sign that reads "Lobster Mtn. 2 miles." From the water, you'll probably first spy a picnic table at Jackson Cove Campsite, which is just east of the trailhead (for you, it should be to the left of the trailhead). At the trailhead is a grassy clearing where you can pull your boat out of the water to leave while you're hiking.

A sign marks the trailhead for the public hiking trail that leads from the shore of Lobster Lake to a viewpoint near the top of Lobster Mountain.

Starting out with a gradual incline through a pretty mixed forest, the trail is clearly marked with blue blazes. As you climb, notice how the forest changes from mostly deciduous trees to dense conifers. This is characteristic of most Maine mountains.

For challenges, expect a few steep sections of trail, as well as some rocky areas where footing can be tricky. Also, there's a stretch of the trail that has been eroded by flowing water and can be difficult to navigate.

A bench, constructed by a Boy Scout group from Connecticut, is situated at the overlook at the end of the trail. From that spot, you can look out over Lobster Lake and the large island in the middle of the lake, Leadbetter Island.

Lobster Mountain was simply named after Lobster Lake, according to the book *Mountains of Maine: Intriguing Stories Behind Their Names* by Steve Pinkham. Lobster Lake received its name from lumbermen and trappers working in the region, but why they named it after a sea creature is debated. Some say that it's because the lake is roughly the shape of a lobster claw. Others claim the name stems from the many lobster-like crayfish that live in the lake.

For more information: Call (207) 529-1153 (Apr through Nov) or (207) 941-4014 (Dec through Mar) or visit www.maine.gov/penobscotrivercorridor, where a printable brochure and trail map is available on the right side of the page, under "Maps."

Derek and Oreo hike along a particularly rocky section of the trail leading up Lobster Mountain.

Personal note: The first time I tried to hike Lobster Mountain was in July of 2017, and I ended up popping a tire and wrecking a rim on my Subaru Forester after stubbornly trying to drive through an impressive washout on the gravel road leading to the boat launch at Lobster Stream.

If at first you don't succeed, pay $400 to get your car fixed and try again. The very next weekend, my husband, Derek, and I, along with our dog, Oreo, headed up to the Moosehead Lake Region again. Worried the washout might not be fixed, we planned for a weekend on the other side of the lake, the east side, and drove to the boat launch on Lobster Stream from that direction. Along the way, the lady manning the Caribou Checkpoint told us that the washout had indeed been fixed.

As Derek fitted a doggy lifejacket on Oreo, I moved our hiking packs around the canoe and placed a few towels down between our seats. It would be Oreo's second time canoeing, and his first experience had been just a short paddle.

"This may be overly ambitious," I said as Derek lifted Oreo into the canoe and held him in place as I shoved the boat off from shore.

Steering into the center of the stream, we worked our way toward Lobster Lake. Oreo whined nervously behind me as I paddled in the bow. Derek steered in the stern, keeping us as far from land as possible. If we got too close, Oreo would likely make a dash for it.

As we worked up the calm stream, a growl and gurgling sound startled me. I turned to find Oreo leaned over the side of the canoe, biting at the water and getting great quantities of it up his nose. I couldn't help but laugh, but we knew his game couldn't last; he was close to upsetting our boat. So we calmed him down and convinced him to lie down. It didn't last long. We were battling with his antics the entire paddle, especially out on the lake, where the small waves and open water made him even more nervous. He kept trying to climb into my lap, and I'm sure his whining was loud enough to annoy the campers along the shore.

Once on the lake, I referred several times to the map we carried, trying to identify landmarks and judge distances. I was able to identify Ogden Point, which we canoed around, noticing several tents, tarps, and boats stationed at campsites along the shore.

Once around the point, we paddled to the south side of the cove and I scanned the shore until I saw a gap in the woods. We headed in that direction, and as we got closer, I excitedly pointed out a trail sign set back from the shore. We'd found the trailhead to Lobster Mountain.

As you can imagine, Oreo was overjoyed to be on dry land. We let him sprint back and forth on the trail as we made our way up the mountain. It started to drizzle, but the dense canopy of the forest protected us and we made it to the outlook atop the mountain just as the clouds were starting to thicken. I took photos of the hazy view, then watched as Lobster Lake disappeared beneath a wall of white.

It then began to pour. Wrapping my camera in my rain jacket, I tucked it in my backpack and we hurried down the mountain. The canopy could no longer protect us. Water poured into my eyes, blurring my vision as I navigated down slippery rocks

The author and Oreo hike along the 2-mile trail on Lobster Mountain.

and tree roots. I wished I'd thought to bring a baseball cap. Derek chuckled when he turned around to see me holding a large leaf over my eyes, pressed to my forehead as a makeshift visor. It actually helped.

Bright yellow mushrooms, piles of moose droppings, giant maple trees, and a loon fishing in the lake—these were highlights of our adventure. But what really made Lobster Mountain such a memorable hike were the challenges we faced and overcame to get there. As we paddled back, the clouds moved off to the east and the late afternoon sun shone through the spruce trees lining Lobster Stream. We drifted, letting the lazy current carry us for a while as we watched a belted kingfisher dart over the water.

Hike 31: Sentinel Mountain in Baxter State Park

Difficulty: Moderate to strenuous. The 6.2-mile hike has a long warm-up section, where you follow a trail around Kidney Pond and through a mossy forest to Sentinel Mountain. The trail then becomes steep as it climbs the mountain to form a loop near the top. Expect the trail to be very rocky and uneven but well maintained and marked. Watch your footing, especially on narrow bog bridges and exposed tree roots, which can be slippery in wet weather.

Dogs: Not permitted

Cost: During the summer, day use of the park for Maine residents is free; for nonresidents, there is an entrance fee of $15 per vehicle. During the winter—usually Dec through Mar, depending on weather—day use of the park is free for everyone. Campsite, cabin, bunkhouse, and group campground rental fees vary and must be registered for in advance.

Access: The park is open to the public year-round, but during the winter, park roads are closed to vehicles and visitors must travel in on foot, snowshoes, or skis. Snowmobiles are permitted on some park roads. Motorcycles, ATVs, and oversize vehicles (more than 9 feet tall, 7 feet wide, or 22 feet long) are not permitted in the park. Most park trails are for foot traffic only. Bicycles are permitted on maintained park roads and the Dwelley Pond Trail, and Dec through Apr, bicycles are permitted on the Abol Stream Trail.

Wheelchair accessibility: The trails were not constructed to be wheelchair accessible.

Hunting: Not permitted

Restrooms: Outhouses are located at the beginning of the hike at the Kidney Pond Campground parking area.

How to get there: Travel on I-95 to exit 244, then turn west on Route 157 and travel through Medway, East Millinocket, and Millinocket. Drive straight through two traffic lights in downtown Millinocket, then bear right at a three-way intersection and then left at the next Y intersection, staying on the main road. (Along the way will be signs directing you to Baxter State Park.) Drive about 16 miles to the Togue Pond Gatehouse. (The blacktop road turns to gravel before the gatehouse.) After registering at the gatehouse, veer left at the Y intersection and drive 10.4 miles, then turn left onto the side road to Kidney Pond Campground. Drive about 0.5 mile to the campground and park in the day-use parking area, which will be to your right and is marked with signs. Start your hike on the Kidney Pond Trail, which begins at the day-use parking area.

GPS coordinates: Trailhead at Kidney Pond Campground, 45.893778, -69.049009

Topping off at 1,842 feet above sea level, Sentinel Mountain is one of the shortest named peaks in Baxter State Park, but from several overlooks near its top, it offers spectacular views of the region, including a front-and-center view of nearby Katahdin, the tallest mountain in Maine. Starting at Kidney Pond Campground, the hike up Sentinel Mountain and back measures 6.2 miles and travels over rugged terrain, with plenty of rocks and tree roots to keep you on your toes.

The hike begins at the Kidney Pond Trailhead, where you should sign the trail register so park rangers know the details of your trip just in case you become lost or injured and need assistance. That being said, all hikes in Baxter State Park are fairly remote, and help may take some time to reach you. Always pack enough water, food,

Sentinel Mountain in Baxter State Park

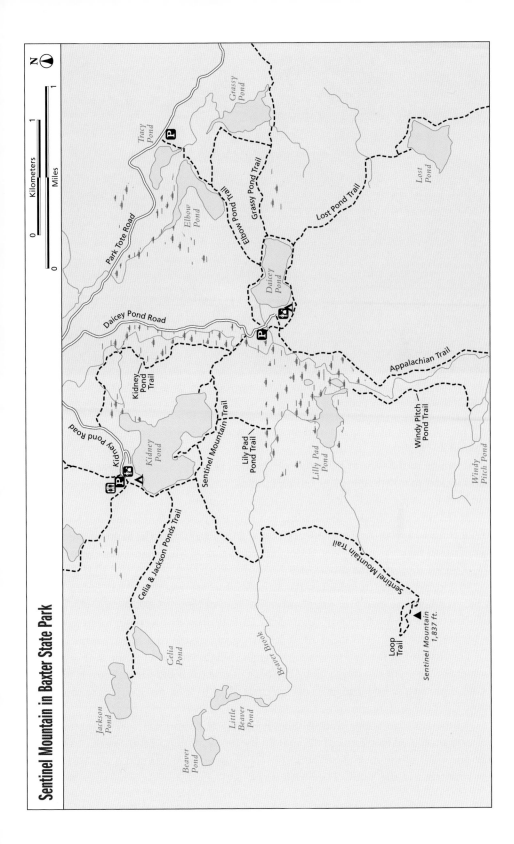

The Sentinel Mountain Trail passes a series of tiny waterfalls near the base of Sentinel Mountain in Baxter State Park.

and provisions to safely spend a night in the woods (even if it's not a particularly comfortable night).

Running to the west of Kidney Pond, the trail kisses the shore in a few locations and includes narrow bog bridges and rocky areas. During this part of the hike, listen and look for loons, which are known to nest on the pond.

At 0.3 mile you'll pass a trail leading to Celia and Jackson Ponds, and at 0.5 mile you'll come to a second intersection. Here you'll turn right onto the Sentinel Mountain Trail to hike toward Beaver Brook and the Sentinel Mountain Loop (which is the 0.6-mile loop atop the mountain).

Striking west, away from Kidney Pond, the Sentinel Mountain Trail winds through a mossy, whimsical stretch of forestland to the base of Sentinel Mountain, which is right on the southwest border of Baxter State Park. Perhaps that accounts for its name, as the landmark appears to stand off on its own, guarding the park like a "sentinel."

The first half of the trail traverses over gentle hills as you travel to the foot of the mountain. The trail also travels along the edge of a wetland and through lovely beds of moss on narrow bog bridges. This is a great place to look for a variety of plants, mosses, lichens, and mushrooms.

A little less than a mile from Kidney Pond, the trail crosses Beaver Brook on a series of small boulders scattered throughout the brook. This is a bit tricky due to the size and angle of the rocks. Use caution while crossing the water, and if you have to get your feet wet, that's OK. The brook isn't deep.

From the brook, the trail starts to climb very gradually at first, then the slope becomes steeper and rockier. Though hand-over-foot climbing is not required, you may find yourself grabbing onto tree trunks for purchase in a few areas.

At 2.3 miles from Kidney Pond, the trail splits into the 0.6-mile Sentinel Mountain Loop, which forms a circle around the top of the mountain, traveling over exposed bedrock and through beds of alpine plants (including lowbush blueberries) to visit several outlooks. If you hike this loop counterclockwise, you'll soon reach a view looking northeast to Katahdin. There is no summit sign.

Covering more than 200,000 acres of mountainous forestland dotted with pristine ponds, Baxter State Park is home to about 215 miles of hiking trails and 337 campsites. The park was pieced together between 1930 and 1962 by former Maine governor Percival P. Baxter, who donated the property to the state so that it could be protected as "forever wild" and open to the public for low-impact recreation such as hiking, paddling, fishing, and camping.

For more information: Visit www.baxterstateparkauthority.com or call the park office at (207) 723-5140.

A series of bog bridges helps hikers minimize impact in a mossy forest edging a wetland at the base of Sentinel Mountain.

A young snowshoe hare sits among the clover at Nesowadnehunk Campground in Baxter State Park in late August.

Personal note: I stumbled out of my tent at 5 a.m. on Saturday in early August and zombie-walked to the pavilion of our group campsite in Nesowadnehunk Field. Baxter Barista John—a camper in our group who has adopted the task of brewing coffee in the morning for everyone to enjoy—handed me a warmed coffee mug and steered me to the coffee dispenser, already loaded with caffeine-filled goodness. Bagels waited on the nearby picnic table.

We would have been rising with the sun, I'm sure, but the thick cloud cover blocked it from view. It wasn't the ideal weather for hiking, but we were determined. One group of hikers from our campground planned to climb Katahdin on the Abol Trail, while another planned to hike the less challenging Sentinel Mountain. I was a part of the second group, and we totaled five hikers in all.

While we had all hiked Katahdin, some of us multiple times, none of us had ever hiked Sentinel Mountain before. That was part of its appeal. I had been told by fellow hikers that the mountain offers spectacular views, but the clouds refused to lift that morning. We hiked the 0.6-mile loop around Sentinel's summit in a cloud. It was a disappointment to not be able to see beyond a few hundred feet, but we didn't let it dampen our spirits. The trail, in and of itself, was beautiful and offered a great workout. The views would have just been a bonus.

Highlights of our hike included a wide variety of interesting mushrooms growing alongside the trail; lush, undisturbed beds of bright green moss carpeting the forest floor; a pile of smashed blueberries that we knew to be black bear scat; clean, cold water forming tiny waterfalls and clear pools beside the trail; wood frogs; granite boulders; and tall trees that sheltered us from the rain.

Hike 32: Trout Brook Mountain in Baxter State Park

Difficulty: Moderate. The 3.3-mile loop hike of Trout Brook Mountain includes long stretches of gradual but constant climbing, as well as a few particularly rocky sections where footing is tricky.

Dogs: Not permitted

Cost: Entry for day use of the park is $15 for nonresidents and free for Maine residents.

Access: Motorcycles are not permitted in the park, and vehicles cannot be more than 9 feet high, 7 feet wide, or 22 feet long. All visitors must register at Matagamon Gate before entering the park. Matagamon Gate is open 6 a.m. to 10 p.m. daily during the summer season, which changes annually depending on snow conditions and mud season. During winter, Matagamon Gate is closed; you would need to park outside the gate and ski or snowshoe 2.6 miles on the unplowed park road to the trailhead for Trout Brook Mountain, making for a much longer and more challenging trip. Camping is permitted at authorized campsites from May 15 to October 15. In the winter, camping sites must be reserved by mail or in person.

Wheelchair accessibility: The trails were not constructed to be wheelchair accessible.

Hunting: Not permitted

Restrooms: Outhouses are located at Trout Brook Farm Campground and at Matagamon Gate.

How to get there: Take I-95 exit 264, then head north on Route 11 toward the town of Patten. Drive 9.3 miles, then take a left onto Route 159. In 9.9 miles you'll arrive at Shin Pond Village, which is a great place to gather any final supplies for the hike. Drive another 14.3 miles, staying on Route 159, to Matagamon Wilderness Campground, then cross a bridge over the East Branch of the Penobscot River. Continue another 1.8 miles to Matagamon Gate, the north entrance to Baxter State Park. Register at Matagamon Gate, then drive 2.6 miles to the trailhead parking area for Trout Brook Mountain, which will be on your left, just after the entrance to Trout Brook Campground, which will be on your right.

GPS coordinates: 46.163661, -68.852183

Rising 1,767 feet above sea level on the north end of Baxter State Park, Trout Brook Mountain features a 3.3-mile loop hike that leads to great views of the nearby Traveler mountains and Grand Matagamon Lake, as well as some lesser mountains and bodies of water. Marked with blue blazes, the hiking trail travels through a number of different forest habitats, featuring a wide variety of plants, mosses, lichens, and mushrooms.

At the trailhead parking area, sign the trail register, then begin your hike on the Trout Brook Mountain Trail, which starts by climbing up a grassy hill and entering a beautiful mixed forest of mostly deciduous trees—maples, birches, beech, and oak. The trail then passes through a stand of large white cedars on its way up the north slope of the mountain. The climb is gradual but steady, and like most of the other hiking trails in Baxter State Park, the trail travels over unimproved forest floor that is uneven due to an abundance of rocks and exposed tree roots. Watch your step.

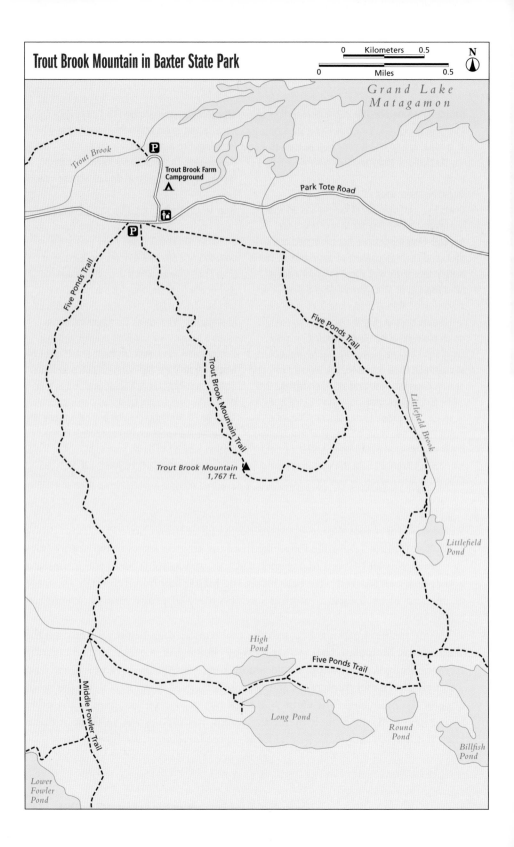

Trout Brook Mountain in Baxter State Park

0   Kilometers   0.5

0   Miles   0.5

N

Grand Lake Matagamon

Trout Brook

P

Trout Brook Farm Campground

Park Tote Road

P

Five Ponds Trail

Five Ponds Trail

Trout Brook Mountain Trail

Littlefield Brook

Trout Brook Mountain 1,767 ft.

Littlefield Pond

High Pond

Five Ponds Trail

Middle Fowler Trail

Long Pond

Round Pond

Billfish Pond

Lower Fowler Pond

An outlook atop Trout Brook Mountain offers a view of Billfish Pond, Billfish Mountain, and Horse Mountain at the north end of Baxter State Park.

About 0.7 mile into the hike, the trail emerges from the forest onto exposed bedrock. Here you'll be rewarded with your first open view of the forest to the north and the long body of Grand Matagamon Lake.

The trail continues up the mountain, then descends into a small dip before climbing to the summit about 1.3 miles from the trailhead. The summit, marked with a wooden sign, is on a small patch of exposed bedrock with a partial view over the treetops. For the best views of the hike, continue on the trail past the summit, south to the ledges on the south side of the mountain. The trail then strikes east, tracing the top of these ledges and offering several open views of the Traveler mountains—which includes The Traveler, North Traveler, and Peak of the Ridges, all rising above 3,000 feet in elevation—as well as the smaller Billfish Mountain and Barrel Ridge. A few tall spruce trees growing on the rocky slope break up the view. Moving diagonally down the slope, the trail reenters the forest about 1.5 miles into the hike.

Moving down the eastern side of the mountain, the trail offers a fairly gentle and constant descent with just a few steep areas. As it nears the base of the mountain, the trail swings north to end at the Five Ponds Trail about 2.3 miles into the hike. Here you'll turn left to hike the final 1.1 miles back to the trailhead parking area, closing the loop. Most of the descent is through a mixed forest of mainly deciduous trees, including aspen, beech, striped maple, birch, and maple trees. Along the way, you'll pass a small meadow and walk through a dense cluster of balsam fir trees.

An outlook about 0.7 mile up the Trout Brook Mountain Trail offers a nice view of Grand Lake Matagamon.

You'll emerge on the east end of the parking area. Don't forget to sign out on the trail register.

Pieced together by former Maine governor Percival P. Baxter between 1931 and 1962, Baxter State Park covers 209,644 acres north of Millinocket. Baxter is home to more than 200 miles of hiking trails that visit pristine ponds, waterfalls, and a number of sizable mountains.

Located in the north end of the park, Trout Brook Mountain is much less crowded than the more popular mountains reached through the south entrance of the park, such as Katahdin. So if you're looking for a quiet, moderately challenging hike with great views, this is a good mountain for you.

For more information: Call (207) 723-5140 or visit www.baxterstatepark.org, where a detailed map of the trails on and around Trout Brook Mountain is available under the tab "Design Your Trip" by selecting "Hike" and "Summer," then scrolling down to the link for the Trout Brook Farm trail map.

Personal note: There's something about a road hemmed in by a thick forest for miles and miles that makes one second-guess oneself.

"Is it supposed to be this far?" my mother, Joyce, asked as she navigated the windy, tree-lined road to the north entrance of Baxter State Park in mid September.

"Trout Brook Campground is 27 miles from Patten," I said, referring to the Appalachian Mountain Club's *Maine Mountain Guide*. "And we haven't gone 27 miles yet."

Meanwhile, my husband, Derek, snoozed in the backseat. He'd come down with a bit of a head cold that morning but insisted he felt well enough to hike, and that the fresh air would do him some good.

At Matagamon Gate, the north entrance of the park, we were greeted by a Baxter attendant who checked us in for the day.

"It wasn't supposed to be like this today," the man said, referring to the clear blue skies and sunshine. The weather report had called for a foggy morning and cloudy afternoon.

"But I'll take it," he continued, adding that it looked like a great day for hiking the Trout Brook Mountain loop.

With the trailhead at Trout Brook Farm Campground—a beautiful field with a brown ranger cabin and campsites tucked into the woods all around—I imagine Trout Brook Mountain is a popular day hike for people camping there. We completed

Derek hikes along the steep south slope of Trout Brook Mountain in September. From the ledges on the south side of the mountain, hikers enjoy views of the nearby Traveler mountains, as well as Billfish Mountain and several ponds.

Derek stands at an outlook on Trout Brook Mountain.

the hike in a little less than three hours, and at the top of the mountain, we were rewarded with a number of different views of the surrounding wilderness.

Throughout the hike, we felt fall's presence. Leaves floated down to rest on the forest floor, maple red and aspen yellow, knocked loose by the breeze; and the rich scent of decaying vegetation triggered my mind to think of pumpkin patches and apple picking.

As we descended the mountain, we took care to step over clusters of yellow mushrooms that seemed to be sprouting up everywhere. We spooked a grouse, which flew just a short distance before touching down again to shuffle through the dry leaves. We also scared a large toad off the trail, walked past a pile of moose droppings, and disturbed a number of squirrels harvesting pinecones.

After completing our hike, we stopped at Shin Pond Village for ice cream cones. And just a warning: The "small" cone isn't small; it's actually quite big—three scoops at least, maybe four. But I won't complain.

Hike 33: Orin Falls in Katahdin Woods and Waters National Monument

Difficulty: Moderate. Most of the 6-mile hike follows an old logging road that travels over gentle hills. At the far end of the hike is a short, narrow footpath that leads over narrow bog bridges and an uneven forest floor to Orin Falls. This traditional hiking trail is only a couple hundred feet long.

Dogs: Permitted if kept on leash

Cost: None

Access: Most of this adventure is open to foot traffic, mountain bikes, and horseback riding, with the final stretch of trail to Orin Falls for foot traffic only. ATVs and snowmobiles are prohibited. The roads leading to the hike are not plowed in the winter. Camping at designated campsites is free—first come, first served—but you'll need to obtain a Maine Forest Service campfire permit to enjoy a campfire, and you'll also need to obtain a permit for overnight parking from the KWW Millinocket Welcome Center at 200 Penobscot Ave. in Millinocket or the Lumberman's Museum at 61 Shin Pond Rd. in Patten.

Wheelchair accessibility: The trails were not constructed to be wheelchair accessible.

Hunting: Not permitted

Restrooms: The nearest outhouse is at the Sandbank Stream campsite and day-use area on the Katahdin Loop Road, approximately 5 miles from the Orin Falls trailhead parking lot.

How to get there: From a bend in Route 11 at the center of Stacyville (a town that is just north of Medway and Millinocket), turn left onto the gravel Swift Brook Road. Reset your odometer. In about 1 mile you'll cross a bridge over Swift Brook. At 5.2 miles veer left to stay on Swift Brook Road. At about the 7-mile mark, you'll cross over the East Branch of the Penobscot River on a long, one-lane bridge high above the water. At 9.8 miles you'll pass the Sandbank Stream Campsite, and at 10.1 miles you'll pass a sign for Katahdin Woods and Waters National Monument by a wetland area. At 12 miles you'll arrive at the beginning of the Katahdin Loop Road. Turn right and reset your odometer. In 1.3 miles turn right onto Orin Falls Road, and drive approximately 2.5 miles to the trailhead parking area. Start your hike by walking past a gate that blocks the old logging road off from vehicular traffic at the far end of the parking lot.

GPS coordinates: 45.924181, -68.705544

The hike—or bike ride—to Orin Falls was one of the first day trips established in the Katahdin Woods and Waters National Monument. Most of the 6-mile, out-and-back hike follows an old logging road, with the last leg of the hike turning onto a narrow woodland trail that leads to the edge of Wassataquoik Stream at Orin Falls, a series of cascades and rapids tumbling around large granite boulders.

From the trailhead at the end of Orin Falls Road, the hike starts at a gate that bars vehicular traffic and follows an old logging road along a glacial esker, which is a ridge of sand and gravel formed by glaciers thousands of years ago. Just a short distance from the trailhead, you'll come to a signed intersection where you'll turn left to hike toward Orin Falls. Shortly after, the International Appalachian Trail (IAT) joins the logging road on your right, where it descends through the woods and crosses

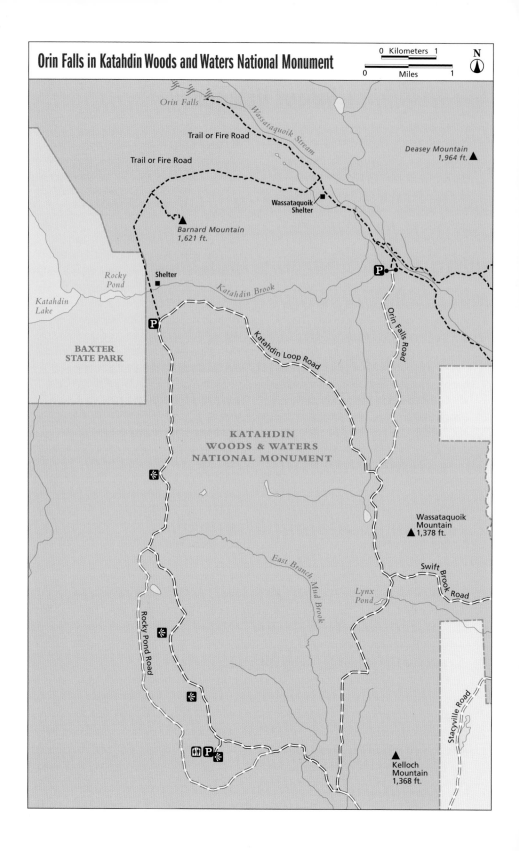

Orin Falls in Katahdin Woods and Waters National Monument

0   Kilometers   1

0   Miles   1

N

Orin Falls

Wassataquoik Stream

Trail or Fire Road

Deasey Mountain
1,964 ft. ▲

Trail or Fire Road

Wassataquoik
Shelter

▲
Barnard Mountain
1,621 ft.

*Rocky
Pond*   Shelter

Katahdin Brook

P

*Katahdin
Lake*

P

Orin Falls Road

BAXTER
STATE PARK

Katahdin Loop Road

KATAHDIN
WOODS & WATERS
NATIONAL MONUMENT

Wassataquoik
Mountain
▲ 1,378 ft.

East Branch Mud Brook

Swift Brook Road

*Lynx
Pond*

Rocky Pond Road

Stacyville Road

🏕 P

▲
Kelloch
Mountain
1,368 ft.

The author walks among large granite boulders scattered throughout Wassataquoik Stream at Orin Falls in August. To capture the photograph, she set up her camera on a boulder and programmed it to take multiple photos on a timer.

Wassataquoik Stream in a fordable location, then travels west and then north to the top of Deasey Mountain (and on to cross the border into Canada).

The IAT is a fairly new trail that is still in development. In a sense, it's a huge expansion to the popular Appalachian National Scenic Trail, which spans from Springer Mountain in Georgia to Katahdin in Maine. Proposed by Maine fisheries biologist Richard Anderson in 1994, the IAT follows the remnants of the Appalachian Mountains across countries and overseas. As of July 2015, there were IAT walking trails in Maine, New Brunswick, Quebec, Nova Scotia, Prince Edward Island, Newfoundland, Greenland, Iceland, Norway, Sweden, Denmark, Scotland, Northern Ireland, Ireland, Isle of Man, Wales, England, France, Spain, Portugal, and Morocco. And the IAT will continue to expand, according to the trail's official website, www.iat-sia.org.

After joining with the IAT, the old logging road leading to Orin Falls descends a gentle hill to an old wooden bridge that spans Katahdin Brook, an outflow from nearby Katahdin Lake in Baxter State Park. Beyond the bridge is the IAT Wassataquoik Campsite that includes a picnic table, a fire ring, and a lean-to that was constructed in 2008 and donated by Katahdin Forest Products.

Past the campsite, the old road passes through a section of hardwood forest where you can find woodland flowers such as trillium and trout lily, according to an interpretive brochure for the Katahdin Loop Road published by Friends of Katahdin Woods and Waters National Monument. Many different birds call this forest home,

Water cascades over boulders and ledges at Orin Falls in Katahdin Woods and Waters National Monument in August.

including the sharp-shinned hawk, scarlet tanager, spruce grouse, northern parula, ovenbird, and a number of different species of warblers.

At the halfway point, about 1.5 miles into the hike, you'll come to an intersection where the IAT turns left onto a logging road, striking west to Barnard Mountain, another popular hike in the national monument. The way to Orin Falls is straight ahead and marked with a sign.

Continuing through the forest—past raspberry and blackberry bushes and clusters of young pine trees and then crossing the boundary from Township 3, Range 8, to Township 4, Range 8—the old road travels over a few gentle hills. At nearly the 3-mile mark, the hike turns right onto a narrow footpath that travels through a mixed forest to the banks of Wassataquoik Stream at Orin Falls. This trail, measuring just a few hundred feet long, is well groomed and marked with a brown sign that reads Orin Falls. It includes a couple narrow bog bridges, a wider wooden bridge, and rock steps.

At the edge of Wassataquoik Stream, named for a Native American word meaning "place where they spear fish," you can rock-hop clear across the stream at low water. Small gravel beaches are scattered along the banks, and large boulders make for great places to sit, picnic, and fish. This location also includes several fairly deep pools situated among the boulders and ledges that make for great swimming holes. And for anglers, brook trout have been found in this stream in recent years.

For more information: Visit www.nps.gov/kaww or www.friendsofkatahdin woodsandwaters.org.

Personal note: A half-squished alien-like bug landed on my chest, its legs still twitching, and I hastily brushed it off.

"That's not the first bug you've thrown at me today, is it?" I asked my BDN coworker John Holyoke as we walked along the old logging road toward Orin Falls on an overcast day in August.

"Nope, and it won't be the last," he said.

To that I grumbled, but in truth, I didn't really mind. John had sat across from me at the BDN office in Bangor for many years, and he always joked around with me. I expected nothing less. And after six years of writing and filming my "1-minute hike" column, he was finally joining me on a hike. It was a big day.

Actually, it was our second hike together that day in the Katahdin Woods and Waters National Monument. We had warmed up with a short hike over an esker and down to a small pond near the south entrance of the property. Feeling good about that, John decided to join me on the longer hike I'd planned to Orin Falls. Carrying

The trail to Orin Falls follows an old woods road that crosses Katahdin Brook on an aged wooden bridge.

Large granite boulders scattered throughout Wassataquoik Stream make for a stunning scene.

his fly rod in a long case tipped onto his shoulder, he walked quickly down the old logging road, trying to outrun the horseflies and mosquitoes.

If you attempt this hike any time from late spring through summer, bring effective bug repellent and cover as much skin as you can bear with clothing. The road dips down into a forest filled with stagnant pools of water that are prime mosquito breeding grounds. I envied John for his baseball cap, which protected his head from the circling deerflies and monstrous horseflies. As it stood, I'd brought all-natural bug repellent, which John at first poo-pooed (saying it probably attracted flies rather than repelled them), then used in copious amounts—as did I.

The destination, we found, was well worth the long walk and itchy bug-bitten legs. Orin Falls, though no great waterfall, was a sight to behold. The clear water of Wassataquoik Stream churned and tumbled around and over granite rocks and boulders that had been rounded by erosion into smooth, organic shapes. Boulders larger than cars were scattered throughout the stream, along with smaller boulders perfect for rock-hopping.

Just minutes after our arrival, the blanket of clouds that had hung over us all morning broke up and sunlight painted the colorful stones of the streambed. A breeze swept upstream, scattering the biting flies, and I was in heaven.

Navigating the rocks, I explored upstream as John sat down to enjoy the view. We lingered there a while, then headed back the way we came, stopping now and then to inspect blueberry-filled bear scat and photograph toads, woods frogs, and garter snakes.

Hike 34: Mount Chase near Patten

Difficulty: Strenuous. The hike is 3.4 miles out and back, and is steep and rocky much of the way.

Dogs: Permitted if kept on leash

Cost: None

Access: The trail is accessible year-round. In the winter, a good portion of the trail is used by snowmobilers.

Wheelchair accessibility: The trails were not constructed to be wheelchair accessible.

Hunting: Only with private landowner permission

Restrooms: None

How to get there: Take I-95 exit 264 and drive north on Route 11 through the towns of Stacyville and Patten. After about 16 miles, turn left onto Mountain Road in the town of Hersey. Drive about 2 miles on this gravel road and park in a small clearing across the road from a picnic table, where you'll find a sign that directs you to continue straight on the road to hike the mountain. Continuing on Mountain Road on foot, the trail up the mountain soon branches off to your right, marked with a sign reading Mt. Trail tucked into the trees, a red arrow spray-painted on a small rock, and orange and pink flagging tape. Be sure to follow the flagging tape.

GPS coordinates: 46.094065, -68.469174

Rising 2,440 feet above sea level, Mount Chase features a steep 1.7-mile trail that leads to the mountain's bald summit, where hikers are rewarded with spectacular open views of the region. The trail is marked with orange and pink flagging tape and a few old signs that can be difficult to read, so it may be wise to carry a GPS device if hiking this mountain for the first time.

Starting at a small clearing near the end of Mountain Road, the trail begins by following the road, then heads into the forest on your right and starts to climb the mountain. The climb starts out fairly gradual but quickly becomes steep and rocky. At 0.8 mile you'll come to a trail intersection with old carved wooden signs that are nearly impossible to read. Continue straight ahead (west) to keep climbing. (Do not take the trail to your right.)

As you climb, you'll be walking through a mostly hardwood forest. The trail, which starts out wide, narrows into more of a traditional hiking trail. If in doubt of which direction to go, simply follow the flagging tape, which is tied to trees all the way to the summit.

A little over a mile into the hike, the trail travels through a grassy area where you'll find a wooden sign that states that Mount Chase summit is in 0.5 mile, and indeed it is. Soon after the sign, you'll come to an old fire warden's cabin, which is still standing but has seen better days. The cabin lacks doors and windows, and the flooring is starting to give way. Explore with caution.

Soon after the cabin, the trail becomes steep and rocky. The final 0.5 mile of the hike is almost a steady climb, with just a few short flat stretches where you can catch your breath. At about 1.5 miles you'll come to an intersection where you can veer

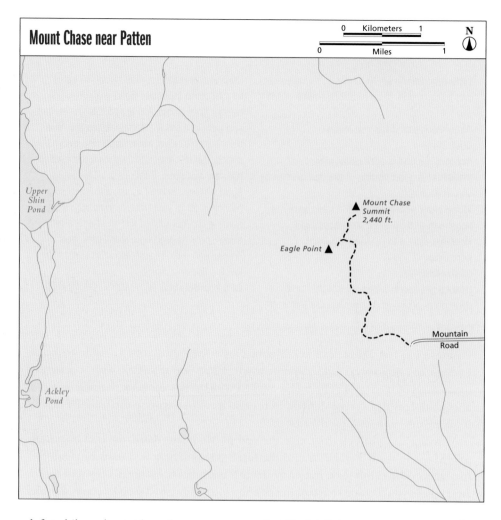

Upper Shin Pond

Mount Chase
Summit
2,440 ft.

Eagle Point ▲

Mountain
Road

Ackley Pond

left to hike a short side trail to an outcrop called Eagle's Point, or you can veer right to complete the last leg of the hike to the summit.

The final 0.2-mile climb is steep and rocky. The trees transition from hardwood to softwood before the trail emerges onto a rocky ridge covered with stunted spruce trees. You'll find no sign at the summit, but you will find a communications building. Just east of that is a metal US Geological Survey marker stamped into the bedrock inside the foundation of an old fire tower. According to the Forest Fire Lookout Association Maine Chapter, the first fire tower on Mount Chase was constructed in 1909, and it was made out of wood. In 1917 that tower was replaced by a steel tower that was 16 feet tall. This tower was relocated to the Patten Lumber Museum in 2001.

From the summit, looking west down the mountain's granite ridge, you'll see a wall of mountains that include nearby Sugarloaf Mountain (not to be confused with

Derek hikes up a rocky section of trail on Mount Chase. ▶

the Sugarloaf Mountain that is home to a ski resort in western Maine), and farther off, the mountains of Baxter State Park, including Katahdin. The bodies of water you can see to the west are Lower Shin Pond and Upper Shin Pond. In all other directions the land is fairly flat, with Pleasant Lake to the north and a few small mountains to the southeast in Island Falls and Oakfield.

For more information: Visit the website of nearby Shin Pond Village at www .shinpond.com, where I initially found directions to the hike, or call (207) 528-2900.

Personal note: The handwritten signs propped up against a picnic table at the trailhead made me grin. This would be an adventure, I told myself. Sometimes the nicest trails are hidden down old dirt roads and marked with such unofficial-looking signs. I wasn't worried; I had a GPS device and my phone had reception, and I knew from a local resident that the trail to the top of Mount Chase was clear. A marathoner, he ran up the trail on a regular basis. (And about half a mile into the hike, as I huffed and puffed, I'd think of that feat—of actually running up the mountain—with awe.)

An old fire warden's cabin stands about 0.5 mile below the summit of Mount Chase by trail.

Derek walks along the ridge of Mount Chase, and beyond him, the sinking sun illuminates Lower Shin Pond.

Sunny with a cool bite of fall in the air, it was the perfect weekend to spend outdoors. Aspen leaves were turning from green to bright yellow, and red was bleeding into the foliage of sugar maples. That evening, my husband and I would stay in a beautiful little log cabin in Mars Hill—about an hour and a half away, nestled between hills and wind turbines on the Canadian border. We'd hike another northern Maine trail the following day.

The hike up Mount Chase started out on a wide, rocky trail that appeared to be an old road that is likely also used by snowmobiles and even ambitious ATVers. The trail remained wide as it traveled through a forest that was neither new nor mature. About a mile into the hike, we commented on how steady a climb it was. I imagine it's the same route the fire warden used to take up the mountain. Fire warden trails are usually fairly direct, without many switchbacks to lessen the slope.

I have to admit that I had no idea there was an old fire warden's cabin on the mountain. There isn't a lot of information about this hike online. So when we arrived at the old, rundown building, I was delighted. Very few fire warden cabins are still standing in Maine. Often they're torn down on state land because they can be a hazard to visitors. And indeed, this particular cabin looks like it might collapse at any moment. Unable to resist, I stepped through the doorless entrance of the cabin to take a few photos of its old stove, cupboards, table, and chair. The walls were covered with the etched names of visitors, which is typical of such cabins, but nevertheless a bit creepy.

We were trying to make good time up the mountain because we'd arrived at the trailhead around 3 p.m. and I'd read that the hike would take one and a half hours. With sundown just after 6 p.m., that was cutting it close. As we hiked the final leg of the trail to the summit, I started to slow down and my dog, Oreo, trotted back to check on me several times. But we made it to the summit in just over an hour, with plenty of sunlight left for our descent.

In fact, by the time we hiked back down to the trailhead, it was dusk, the perfect time for spotting a moose. As we drove away from the mountain on Mountain Road, we passed a wetland, and there at the edge of the water was a big bull moose. Standing a good distance from the road, the moose wasn't at all disturbed when I stepped out of the truck to take a few photos.

A bull moose stands at the edge of a wetland in late September in the northern Maine town of Mount Chase.

Hike 35: Scopan Mountain near Presque Isle

Difficulty: Moderate. The loop trail gradually climbs and descends Scopan Mountain, traveling over unimproved forest floor that includes plenty of roots and some rocks. Stone staircases help hikers gain purchase and climb (or descend) the few steep sections of the trail. The hike is 3.7 miles total.

Dogs: Permitted if kept under control at all times

Cost: None.

Access: Scopan Public Reserved Land is open to all sorts of outdoor activities, including ATVing and snowmobiling, but the hiking trail on Scopan Mountain was constructed for foot traffic only, year-round. Campsites are located nearby on the shores of Scopan Lake.

Wheelchair accessibility: The trails were not constructed to be wheelchair accessible.

Hunting: Permitted in accordance with state laws

Restrooms: An outhouse is available at the trailhead parking area.

How to get there: From the intersection of State Street and Route 163 in downtown Presque Isle, drive west 7 miles on Route 163 (which starts out as Mechanic Street, then turns into Industrial Street, then Mapleton Road) to Mapleton, then turn left onto W. Chapman Road. Reset your odometer. In 5.9 miles W. Chapman Road turns from pavement to gravel. Continue on the gravel road, and in 8.6 miles turn right. Reset your odometer. At 0.4 mile veer right at the fork. At 1.3 miles there will be a road on your left; stay straight. The parking lot is on the left at the 1.9-mile mark.

GPS coordinates: 46.587838, -68.179558

Located within the state-owned Scopan Public Reserved Land just west of Presque Isle, 1,400-foot-high Scopan Mountain features a beautiful 3.7-mile loop hike that leads to the edge of a marsh, then gradually climbs the slope of the mountain to a few partial outlooks of the area's farmlands, forests, and lakes. Marked with blue blazes, the trail is easy to follow and travels through a magnificent old-growth forest filled with big hemlocks, maples, balsam firs, and birches.

Starting at the trail's fairly large gravel parking area, the Scopan Mountain Trail enters the woods to the right of a trailhead kiosk that displays a trail map and some signs reminding visitors not to litter or kindle fires on the property. At the beginning of the trail is a small wooden bench, and just a short distance into the woods, the trail splits into a loop that can be hiked in either direction.

If you veer right and hike the trail counterclockwise, you'll have a good stretch of fairly even terrain where you can warm up and stretch your legs as you hike along the base of the mountain on its east side. About 0.5 mile into the hike, you'll come to a partial view of a beautiful wetland where you'll likely spot some wildlife. In fact, moose are commonly spotted in this area, munching on aquatic plants.

After the outlook, the trail turns east, away from the wetland, and starts climbing gradually up the east side of the mountain. A little over a mile into the hike, you'll come to a long stone staircase that helps you up a steep section of the trail. At about 1.8 mile you'll come to a gap in the trees that offers a view to the east of Alder Lake

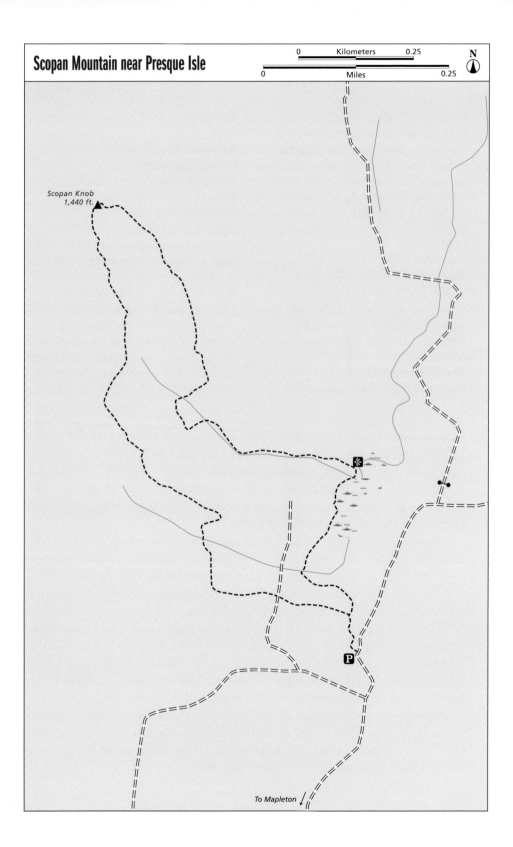

Scopan Mountain near Presque Isle

Kilometers
0 0.25

Miles
0 0.25

N

Scopan Knob
1,440 ft.

P

To Mapleton

A view opens up on the west side of the ridge of Scopan Mountain just southwest of Presque Isle.

and nearby farmland. About 0.1 mile beyond that, you'll come to a second partial view, also of Alder Lake. At this viewpoint is a small wooden bench.

Just a few hundred feet past this view, you'll hit the highpoint of the trail at approximately 1,400 feet above sea level. This is exactly 2 miles into the hike. The actual summit of the mountain is just a bit higher, to the north, but the trail doesn't cross it. Instead, the trail turns and starts to head very gradually down the mountain's south side, where you'll soon come to a view of the forestland west of the mountain.

After the view, the trail continues down the mountain, then climbs up over a small hump before continuing the gradual descent. At 3.6 miles you'll return to the beginning of the loop, where you'll turn right to hike the final 0.1 mile to the trailhead parking lot.

In addition to a hiking trail, the 16,700-acre Scopan Unit contains water-access campsites on the shores of Scopan Lake, where fishing and motorized boating are permitted, and there are additional trails that are open to snowmobiles, ATVs, and cross-country skiing.

For more information: Visit www.maine.gov/scopan or call the Maine Bureau of Parks and Lands northern office in Ashland at (207) 435-7963.

Personal note: The sun shone bright on the beautiful Saturday in September when my husband, Derek, and I hiked Scopan Mountain with our dog, Oreo. At the base of the mountain, some of the leaves were just starting to show their fall colors. Following fresh-painted blazes, we hiked the loop counterclockwise, visiting the marsh and then heading up the mountain.

It's difficult to put a finger on what makes a landscape especially beautiful to me. It's often a combination of things. When it comes to the forest on Scopan Mountain, it was the old hemlock trees towering overhead, their big trunks lined up along the trail. It was the clumps of ferns and young balsam firs, the dead leaves crunching under our boots, and the moose maple leaves fading into yellows so pale they appeared white—big white leaves shining in the sun.

The drumming of a hairy woodpecker drew my attention to where it hopped along the branch of a tree, pausing every now and then to thrust its sharp beak into the bark in search of bugs. Continuing on the trail, I skirted around a pile of moose droppings, then knelt down to inspect an interesting group of tree mushrooms called red-banded polypore for the red-orange band that decorates its half-moon shelf.

A rock staircase runs up a steep slope on Scopan Mountain.

Derek and Oreo walk along a hiking trail on Scopan Mountain.

Atop the mountain, the views were a nice addition to the adventure, but I would have been happy with the hike even if there had been no views at all. This particular hike was less about any single destination and more about the overall journey, which was lovely every step of the way.

Index

Acknowledgments

It's a daunting task to recall how many family members, friends, colleagues, and complete strangers helped me—either directly or indirectly—produce this guidebook. While I hiked the trails, wrote the words, and snapped the photos in this book, it wouldn't have been possible without the support of many people, from the trail builders and stewards throughout the state of Maine to my most devoted hiking companions, my husband, Derek, and our dog, Oreo.

I'd like to acknowledge the *Bangor Daily News* and Down East Books in particular for working with me to make this guidebook a reality. Thank you, Michael Steere from Down East Books for offering me this opportunity, and Kristen Mellitt from Globe Pequot for editing and improving the entire manuscript. At the *Bangor Daily News*, I'd like to give a special thanks to my editor, Sarah Walker Caron, and my fellow writer John Holyoke, who have always been champions of my outdoor writing and photography.

I'd also like to thank my mother, Joyce Clark Sarnacki, who helped edit drafts and offered advice when I needed it most. She also joined me on a number of the hikes, as did my mother-in-law, Geneva Perkins, and friends Gail Purinton White, Jim White, and Lacey Sinclair.

This also seems like the place to point out that without the many organizations and government agencies working hard to conserve wild places in Maine, we wouldn't have so many public trails to enjoy. Those who have painted blazes on trees, erected trail signs, built cairns, cleared brush off trails, and sat in offices doing piles of paperwork to acquire grants to conserve land or fund trail work, I thank you from the bottom of my heart.

Last and perhaps most importantly, I'd like to thank all the people who have read my BDN column, blog, and outdoor-related stories over the years. Your amazing support was nothing I ever expected. You've encouraged me to keep going, to lace up my boots and hike that next trail on my list. When I doubted the merits of my work, your positive feedback and helpful suggestions pushed me forward and up the next mountain. So thank you. Without you, I wouldn't have achieved my dream to write a guidebook, and now, a second.

About the Author

Aislinn Sarnacki is a reporter for the *Bangor Daily News* (BDN), a major news outlet in Maine, writing chiefly for the Outdoors section. Her beat for the news includes outdoor recreation, wildlife, and conservation. And for about six years, she wrote a weekly column about trails, documenting nearly 300 hiking locations throughout the state with text, photographs, and videos.

A lifelong Maine resident, Aislinn grew up in Winterport, a small town located on the Penobscot River. While earning a degree in journalism from the University of Maine in Orono, she was awarded Highest Honors for her thesis, which explored the health benefits of hiking.

In 2012 Aislinn was the recipient of the Bob Drake Young Writer's Award, which is presented each year to a journalist with less than two years' experience whose work demonstrates ability and great potential. More recently the Maine Press Association named her the top features and lifestyle blogger in Maine for 2014 and 2016.

Aislinn and her husband, Derek, along with their dog, Oreo, and two cats, Bo and Arrow, live on a wooded hill overlooking a lake in the Bangor area. This is her second guidebook. The first, *Family Friendly Hikes in Maine,* was published by Down East Books in 2017.

Visit her BDN blog at actoutwithaislinn.com and her personal website and blog at aislinnsarnacki.com.